CREATING A HOME

CREATIVE HOME
DECORATING

WARD LOCK

CONTENTS

5	Introduction
7	Preparing walls
11	Interior paints
13	Painting walls and ceilings
17	Preparing and painting woodwork
21	Special effects with paint
25	Colour washing and shading
29	Speckled paint effects
33	Marbled paint effects
37	Imitating tortoiseshell
41	Paint effects on wood
45	Painting straight lines
49	Using ready-made stencils
53	Making your own stencils
57	Painting murals
61	Hanging wallpaper
65	Decorating ceilings
69	Hanging relief wallcoverings
73	Wallcoverings
75	Cornices and covings
79	Fixing fabric to walls
83	Basic tiling
87	Tiling a work surface
91	Tiling a room
95	Index/Photographic credits

© Ward Lock Limited 1988
Villiers House, 41-47 Strand, London WC2N 5JE, a Cassell Company
Reprinted 1989, 1990, 1992(Twice), 1994
Based on *Creating a Home*,
First Edition © Eaglemoss Publications Limited, 1986

ISBN 0 7063 6723 5

Printed in Spain by Cayfosa Industria Grafica

INTRODUCTION

Decorating your home yourself can be richly
rewarding. Not only does it save money, it gives
you a unique opportunity to exercise your practical and
creative skills.

Designed to help you in both practical and creative
areas, this book shows how to master basic skills, then
develop them to be really adventurous in the way you
decorate your home. All the techniques are explained in
easy-to-follow, step-by-step form, with numerous
drawings and photographs showing the wonderful
effects which you can achieve. Every project includes a
'shopping list' of tools and materials to make sure that
you have everything you need before starting work.

The sections on preparation, painting and paper-hanging
show how to get really professional results with the
minimum of effort. Guides to choosing paints and
wallcoverings include all the latest developments so you
can be sure of picking the best product for your
purpose. And the chapters on ceramic tiling start off
with step-by-step instructions for making a simple
splashback before taking you on to tackle a kitchen
worktop or retile your bathroom.

Creative Home Decorating is a rich source of ideas
for unusual ways of decorating: not only walls, ceilings
and woodwork but furniture too. There are chapters
devoted to the newly popular traditional decorative
techniques such as marbling, ragging, colour washing and
shading, spattering, dragging and combing. Or you can
create your own patterns by stencilling, painting a mural,
or covering your walls with pleated fabric.

Creative Home Decorating is full of bright ideas for
creative original touches, speeding up the work and
saving money. It is a must for everyone who wants to
do their own decorating and do it with flair.

PREPARING WALLS

Take the time to prepare the surface thoroughly and you'll be repaid with a finish that looks good and lasts.

The ideal surface for a decorative finish – paint, paper or tiles – is one that is sound, flat, clean and dry. Dirt and grease will prevent any decorative finish from sticking properly.

The preparatory work that is necessary will depend on the condition of existing surfaces as well as the finish intended for it.

New walls New plaster does not need any special preparation. If walls are still drying out, however, salt crystals may appear on the surface as a white powdery deposit. Brush it off dry and decorate when it stops reappearing. Lightly sand areas of rough plaster with fine-grade abrasive paper and use emulsion paint only so that the plaster can breathe. Do not decorate with anything that is impervious to water

vapour – such as oil-based paint or washable wallpapers – for at least three months.

Painted walls For many painted surfaces a thorough cleaning is all that is required before painting or papering. If there are cracks and holes they should be filled, and any mould growth should be destroyed.

However, distemper, which is sometimes found in old houses, is difficult to decorate over successfully and should always be removed. Test the surface by rubbing with your finger – if the paint comes off easily it is a distemper-type finish.

Textured paint finishes can be painted over but must be removed if you want to use any other material. If the finish is a textured emulsion, you

can soften it with a steam stripper. Otherwise you will have to use a chemical paint remover.

Papered walls Avoid papering or painting over old wallcoverings – the dyes in the old paper may bleed through fresh paint, and adhesive for a new wall-covering may pull both old and new papers from the wall.

Only leave if the paper is stuck to the wall well or the plaster beneath is in such poor condition that it might pull away if you strip the surface (test a small patch first). Prime before painting or hang lining paper for a new wallcovering.

Making the best of it Surfaces that you cannot make smooth but are otherwise sound benefit from a covering of lining paper. Relief papers and textured paint are also useful for disguising uneven and cracked plaster.

Before you start Preparatory work is a messy business, so clear away as many furnishings as possible and pile the rest in the middle of the room under dust sheets. Take down curtains and protect the floor with plastic sheeting.

A perfect finish
A successful decorating job – like this one – depends on thorough preparation of the wall surfaces.

TOOLS AND EQUIPMENT

A sponge or a rough cloth is necessary for washing down surfaces. Use a scrubbing brush on textured paint finishes.

Sugar soap or household detergent will remove dirt and grease from painted surfaces. You will also need a bucket.

Abrasive paper – use wet-and-dry for painted surfaces, ordinary glasspaper for smoothing filled areas. It is useful to have three grades – fine, medium and coarse.

A sanding block helps to give an even finish – improvise by wrapping abrasive paper round a block of wood.

Textured-paint remover may be necessary to remove a textured finish. This can, however, be very expensive.

Washing-up liquid or proprietary wall-paper stripper is used when soaking wallpaper for stripping.

A steam stripper can be hired from a tool hire shop to speed up the process of stripping textured paint and layers of old wallpaper.

A flat scraper with a broad blade is used for stripping wallpaper and paint.

A stiff wire brush, or a scraper with a serrated wire edge, is used to score stubborn wallpapers before soaking with water.

All-purpose filler is available ready-mixed for filling small cracks and holes. Use an interior grade.

A filling knife with a narrow flexible blade is necessary for filling cracks and holes in plaster.

A hammer and cold chisel is useful for removing damaged plaster.

All-purpose plaster – this is available ready-mixed for repairing small areas of damage.

A trowel with a thin flexible blade is necessary for applying plaster.

Plaster finish is essential as a topcoat for new plaster. It comes ready-mixed, and a plastic spreader for application is usually supplied.

An old, clean paintbrush is useful for cleaning out cracks and holes, and dusting off surfaces.

Household bleach, or a proprietary mould killer, is essential for destroying mould on wall surfaces.

You will also need dust sheets and plastic sheeting to protect vulnerable surfaces.

CHECK YOUR NEEDS
- ☐ Plastic bucket
- ☐ Sugar soap or detergent
- ☐ Sponge, cloth or scrubbing brush
- ☐ Clean cloths for wiping down
- ☐ Abrasive paper (wet-and-dry for painted surfaces, ordinary glass-paper for bare plaster)
- ☐ Sanding block
- ☐ Flat scraper
- ☐ Textured paint remover
- ☐ Protective clothing and rubber gloves
- ☐ Old paintbrushes
- ☐ Washing-up liquid or proprietary wallpaper stripper
- ☐ Wire brush or serrated scraper
- ☐ Steam stripper (optional)
- ☐ Interior-grade all-purpose filler
- ☐ Narrow filling knife (25mm blade)
- ☐ Hammer and cold chisel
- ☐ All-purpose plaster
- ☐ Wide filling knife (75mm blade)
- ☐ Plasterer's trowel
- ☐ Plaster finish
- ☐ Bleach or proprietary mould killer

Clean painted walls
Use a sponge (or soft scrubbing brush for textured finishes) and a solution of warm water and sugar soap or household detergent.

Wash the ceiling first, then the walls, working from the bottom upwards to catch any dirty streaks that run down. Rinse thoroughly with clean water and allow to dry.

Then, if the walls have been gloss-painted, rub them down with wet-and-dry abrasive paper to provide a key for new decorations (a fine-grade paper if you're painting; a coarser grade if you are hanging wallpaper).

Remove distemper
Scrub the walls with a firm scrubbing brush and plenty of warm water, changing the water whenever it becomes cloudy. Rinse down with warm water and let the surface dry.

Then sand smooth and apply a stabilizing primer if you are painting or a thin coat of size (weak wallpaper paste) if you are hanging paper.

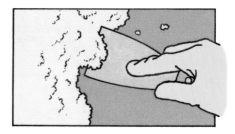

Remove flaking paint △
Use a flat scraper to scrape away small areas of loose flaking paint. Sand the edges of bare patches smooth with fine-grade glasspaper, and paint them with emulsion before repainting the entire wall.

Strip textured paint finishes ▷
A steam stripper may soften the paint sufficiently for stripping in the same way as for wallpaper.

If this fails, use a proprietary textured paint remover. Apply it carefully with a brush, and wear rubber gloves and protective clothing to guard against splashes. Leave the remover to penetrate, then strip off the softened material with a flat scraper and rinse the surface thoroughly with cold water.

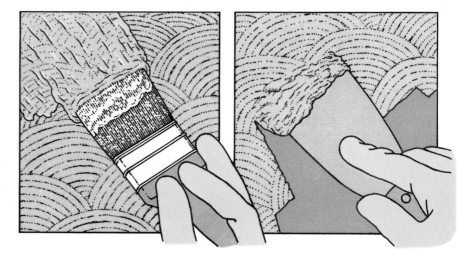

Strip ordinary wallpaper ▷
Use a sponge or old paintbrush to wet the wall with hot water containing a little washing-up liquid or proprietary wallpaper stripper (see Safety note). Leave it to soak through the paper and soften the paste beneath.

Then slide a flat scraper under a loose edge and scrape off the paper. Hold the scraper firmly and keep it as flat to the wall as possible so that you don't dig into the plaster. Keep re-soaking the paper until it comes off easily. To avoid trampling soggy paper around, gather up strippings as you go.

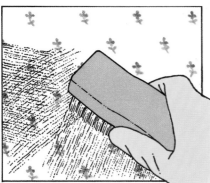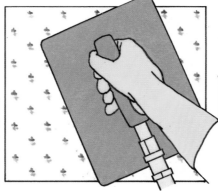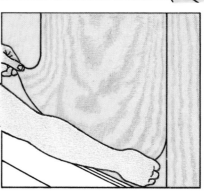

Strip washable or painted paper △
If wallpaper has a water-resistant finish the surface must be broken before sponging to allow the water to soak through. Use a stiff wire brush or a serrated scraper to score the paper, taking care not to damage the surface beneath.

Steam stripper △
You can hire a steam stripper from your local hire shop. This machine forces steam into the paper and speeds up the process of softening the paste – the paper is then scraped off as for ordinary wallpaper. Be sure to follow the hire company's instructions for use carefully.

Strip vinyl wallcoverings △
Peel the top vinyl layer off the backing paper which is stuck to the wall – lift a corner seam with your fingernail at skirting board level, loosen the bottom edge from the wall and pull upwards to remove it completely. You can paint or paper over the backing paper as long as it is firmly stuck to the wall, but for a thorough job it is best to strip it.

◁ **Strip for action**
It really is worth putting the time into preparing your wall surfaces properly. After all, the final finish can only be as smooth as the surface beneath it.

This room is being stripped right back to the basics. Unless old wallpaper is really well stuck to the wall, or the plaster beneath it is in very poor condition, the old paper should be removed before redecorating with new paint or paper.

Getting rid of old wallcoverings usually depends on soaking the walls thoroughly with water so that the adhesive behind the paper begins to dissolve. This is a messy job so clear out as much furniture as possible, take down curtains and, if possible, remove the floorcovering as well.

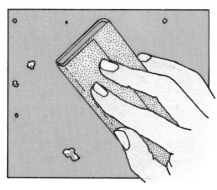

Clean up a stripped surface △
Once all the paper has been removed, rub off any small nibs of paper with coarse-grade glasspaper wrapped around a wood block. Then wash the whole wall with detergent solution to remove old pastes, rub down with fine glasspaper and dust off.

Fill small cracks and holes ▷
Most minor cracks and holes can be dealt with using an interior general-purpose filler. A badly-cracked ceiling, however, can be difficult to fill satisfactorily – wallpaper or textured paint may be a better answer than filling.

Use an all-purpose filler to fill small cracks and holes in walls. First rake out loose material from cracks with the edge of a filling knife and dust off with an old paintbrush. Then wet the plaster with a sponge to stop the repair from drying out too quickly (a houseplant spray comes in handy!).

For cracks, draw the blade across and then along the crack to force the filler well in. Fill a deep crack or hole in 2 or 3 layers of no more than 3mm thickness, allowing each layer to dry

hard before applying the next one. Always overfill the crack or hole – you can rub off the excess with glasspaper once it has dried. Then dust clean with an old paintbrush.

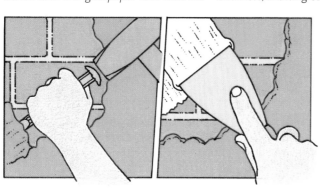

Repair damaged plaster △
Larger holes and areas of damaged plaster up to 30cm square should be repaired with all-purpose plaster and a plaster finish. Leave larger areas of plasterwork to a professional.

Remove damaged material using a hammer and cold chisel (left), working from the centre outwards until you reach sound plaster. Then repair the patch with all-purpose plaster built up in at least two layers to within about 3mm of the surface.

Stir the plaster, then apply it to the wall with a trowel or large filling knife (right). Push the plaster firmly against the wall and spread it smooth, moving the trowel steadily upwards with the blade at an angle of about 45 degrees to the surface. When the first layer begins to harden, roughen up the surface with wire or a nail to provide a key for the next layer.

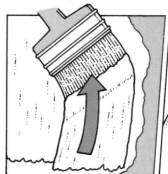

Apply the plaster finish △
Leave the undercoat of plaster for at least twenty-four hours to dry thoroughly before applying a thin 'skim' coat of plaster finish. Stir the plaster until creamy and apply it evenly to the wall using a large paint brush and light upward strokes.

Then smooth over with the flexible plastic spreader provided. Keep working the surface with the spreader until you are satisfied that the finish is smooth. If necessary, dip the spreader into water and slightly dampen the plaster – but only just enough to remove any ridges and marks.

TREATING MOULD

Mould growth – usually black or dark brown splodges on wall surfaces – is encouraged by damp and condensation. In these conditions it can spread rapidly – by airborne spores or even by contact with cleaning cloths that have been previously infected.

Mould can be treated with a solution of household bleach, or with a proprietary mould killer (following the manufacturer's instructions). This will destroy mould but you should also try and take action to avoid re-infection. Increasing heat or insulation and improving ventilation, for example, may be the simplest solutions to a

condensation problem.
Household bleach To use household bleach, make up a solution of 1 part bleach to 5 parts water. Brush it on to infected and surrounding areas and leave to soak overnight. Then scrape off the mould, and burn all the scrapings. Rinse the surface with clean water and apply a fresh bleach solution. Leave for at least three days before decorating.

For mould on wallpaper, remove the infected paper before treating the wall with bleach solution. Use a fungicidal paste when hanging new paper.

After treating mould, sterilise cleaning equipment with bleach.

TOUCH UP FILLED AREAS

A patch of filler or an area of new plaster will absorb far more paint than the surrounding surface area of old plaster. The patched areas will appear slightly grey under a fresh coat of paint.

To avoid this, seal the repair with all-purpose primer or one or two coats of emulsion paint before painting the entire wall.

See Interior Paints, pages 11-12, for information on choosing primers and paints for interior use.

INTERIOR PAINTS

Paint is a decorative and long-lasting protective finish for almost any surface – as long as you choose the right paint for the job.

This chapter deals with paint for indoors, where it is mainly used as a decorative finish. In many homes, colour schemes for a room are quite likely to be changed before the paintwork deteriorates. There are situations, however, where special qualities are needed: paint on kitchen and bathroom walls, for example, has to stand up to condensation and be easy to clean.

Apart from colour, there are two major factors to bear in mind when choosing paint – the type and the finish.

TYPES OF PAINT

Paints are divided into two basic categories: water-based and oil-based paints. The charts below and overleaf tell you where and how to best use them.

Water-based paints (emulsions) include paints referred to as acrylics and vinyls. They are the most simple to work with: no undercoat is required, they are easy to apply, fast-drying, and tools can be cleaned in water. Most emulsions are washable.

Oil-based paints need careful application, and most require cleaning up with white spirit (or similar solvent). They take time to dry, and on bare surfaces both primer and undercoat are essential. They are more expensive but much tougher than emulsion – they are scrubbable and stand up well to moisture and condensation so are ideal for kitchens and bathrooms.

FINISHES

Emulsions are available in matt, silk or textured finishes. Oil-based paints range from a subdued sheen to hard, high gloss.

Paints with a shine, including silk emulsion, will highlight any surface defects but they are much easier to clean than matt.

COLOUR

Most paint finishes are available in a huge range of colours – either ready-mixed or custom-mixed from in-store tinting systems. Colour squares on shade cards are only an approximation of final paint colours, and they're so small that it is hard to imagine how they will look on an expanse of wall. So, before making a decision, try and get small 'test' pots of the colours you like and experiment. Then you can see how they work and avoid making expensive mistakes.

If you are going to have paint custom-mixed, make sure you buy all you need in one batch – getting a precise colour match from a second batch is difficult.

Before splashing out on your tin of paint, check the charts below and overleaf to find out which paint to buy for the job. If necessary, buy solvent at the same time.

THE RIGHT PAINT FOR THE SURFACE

	PRIMER	UNDERCOAT	TOPCOAT
WALLS/CEILINGS			
New plaster/plasterboard	one sealing coat of thinned emulsion OR alkali-resisting primer	not needed / only under liquid gloss	1 or 2 coats of emulsion OR 1 or 2 coats of oil-based paint
	do not use oil-based paint on plaster which has not dried out thoroughly		
Sound painted plaster	thinned coat of emulsion on bare areas OR alkali-resisting primer	not needed	1 or 2 coats of emulsion OR oil-based paint
	do not not use emulsion over gloss paint – it will not bond		
Lining paper/anaglypta	sealing coat of thinned emulsion if using oil-based paint	only under liquid gloss	1 or 2 coats of emulsion OR oil-based paint
Glazed tiles	thinned coat of oil-based Full Gloss paint (9 parts paint: 1 part white spirit)	do not use undercoat	1 coat of oil-based Full Gloss paint
WOOD			
Bare softwood/building boards	knotting over resinous streaks or knots, then wood primer	only under liquid gloss	1 or 2 coats of oil-based paint
Bare hardwood	wood primer	only under liquid gloss	1 or 2 coats of oil-based paint
Sound painted wood	not needed	only under liquid gloss	1 or 2 coats of oil-based paint
METAL			
New galvanized iron (some window frames for example)	quick-drying metal primer or calcium plumbate (contains lead)	undercoat	1 or 2 coats of oil-based paint
Radiators	quick-drying metal primer on bare metal	do not use undercoat	2 coats of oil-based paint

CHOOSING THE RIGHT PAINT

TYPE	USES	ADVANTAGES	WATCH POINTS	SOLVENT/THINNER
Primer Types include: all-purpose wood quick-drying metal calcium plumbate alkali-resisting	Essential on new wood and metal. All-purpose primer is suitable for most surfaces around the home. Other primers available for specific uses.	Seals the surface and provides a key for next coat. Primer on its own is not permanent protection – cover with undercoat and topcoat as quickly as possible.	Calcium plumbate is the best primer for new galvanised metal but it contains lead which could be harmful – use quick-drying metal primer instead.	white spirit
Undercoat	Use after primer when building up a paint system on new wood or metal, or on old paintwork when changing colour significantly. (Not always necessary under non-drip gloss or eggshell.)	Designed to have good covering power; can easily be rubbed smooth ready for a top coat.	Undercoat, like primer, must be painted over as quickly as possible.	white spirit
WATER-BASED PAINTS				
Matt vinyl emulsion liquid solid emulsion	For walls and ceilings. Being water-based they allow surface to breathe so use on new plaster or porous surfaces such as rough brickwork.	Covers well; reflects little light so will not highlight imperfections on uneven walls. Cheap, easy to apply, fast drying (recoatable in about 4 hours), and washable. Solid emulsion non-drip so particularly useful for ceilings.	Shows scuff marks and likely to develop sheen with washing so best used in areas of light wear such as bedrooms, living rooms, dining rooms.	soap and water/water
Silk vinyl emulsion liquid solid emulsion	For walls and ceilings – as for matt vinyl emulsion.	Tougher and more washable than matt vinyl emulsion. Particularly effective on relief papers and other textured wallcoverings. Cheap, easy to apply, fast drying (recoatable in about 4 hours). Solid emulsion non-drip so useful for ceilings.	Will highlight irregular surfaces.	soap and water/water
Textured paint	For walls and ceilings.	Gives a rough-stone finish good for disguising imperfect walls.	Difficult to wash and very difficult to remove.	soap and water/water
Gloss	Interior woodwork.	Easier to apply than oil-based gloss (recoatable in about 6 hours).	Not as hardwearing nor as shiny as oil-based gloss.	soap and water/water
OIL-BASED PAINTS				
Eggshell **Silthane silk**	All-purpose paint for walls and ceilings, wood and metal. Ideal for areas of heavy condensation such as kitchens and bathrooms.	Tougher than emulsion and more subtle than full gloss. Wears well and very washable. Normally needs no undercoat (though bare surfaces should be primed) and needs less brushing out than gloss.	More expensive than emulsion. Takes 12-16 hours to dry and needs more careful application than emulsion.	white spirit
Full gloss non-drip liquid	For surfaces that need maximum protection – kitchen cupboards, window sills and other woodwork. Easy to clean and hardwearing. Non-drip needs no mixing and there's less chance of splashes and runs than with liquid gloss. Applied quite thickly which can mean fewer coats and good covering power. Liquid gloss flows on evenly and is particularly good for difficult surfaces such as window frames and mouldings.	Takes 12-16 hours to dry. The shiny finish highlights surface flaws so thorough preparation is necessary. Non-drip is slightly more expensive than liquid. Liquid gloss is more difficult to use for beginners, needs an undercoat.	white spirit

PAINTING WALLS AND CEILINGS

Brighten up your room with a fresh coat of paint. Or give it a completely new look by sponging on a decorative paint finish in two or more colours.

Painting is the easiest, the least expensive and the most versatile way of giving a room new life.

Paints are available in several finishes and there are literally hundreds of colours to choose from. This chapter deals with water-based emulsion paints and oil-based paints suitable for painting walls and ceilings. Use them for either plain or decorative finishes.

Sponging is the simplest decorative paint treatment to try first.

Where to start Begin with smooth, clean surfaces and your paintwork will look better and last longer. If wall surfaces are very poor, you can paper the walls first with a 'white' paper that is intended for painting over – lining paper or relief paper, for example. To get your walls in good shape, see the chapters on Preparing Walls and Hanging Wallpaper.

Before starting to paint, clean the room to remove dust and make sure that vulnerable surfaces are covered with dust sheets or plastic sheeting.

What to paint first If you are painting the whole room, tackle the ceiling first, then the walls and finally the woodwork.

If you're wallpapering, do all your painting first – then there's no worry about splashing the finished walls.

Which paint? Most people opt for water-based emulsion – it's easy to handle and very fast drying. Solid emulsion is particularly good for ceilings as it doesn't drip.

For kitchens and bathrooms, where condensation may be a problem, an oil-based paint is a practical choice but it needs more careful painting and is slower drying.

See Interior Paints for how to choose the most suitable paint and finish for the job in hand.

How much paint? Two coats of paint are usually sufficient to cover a wall or ceiling. But if the walls are very rough or porous, or you're painting a light colour over a dark one, you may need a third coat to get a good finish.

To calculate the area of walls to be painted, multiply the width of each wall by its height and add the totals together. The ceiling area of a room is usually equal to the floor area (multiply the room's length by its width).

Covering capacity varies from one paint brand to the next but, as a rough guide, 1 litre of emulsion will cover about 12sq m. Check on the paint tin and bear in mind the number of coats which will be needed.

Perfect paintwork
The walls and ceiling of this bright kitchen are painted with oil-based silthane silk which is easier to clean than matt emulsion.

CHECK YOUR NEEDS

☐ Paint

For walls and ceilings:
☐ Roller (lambswool or mohair) *or*
  100mm wall brush *or*
☐ 225 × 100mm paint pad

For filling in edges:
☐ 25mm paint brush *or*
  Edging paint pad

☐ Dust sheets or plastic sheeting for
  floors and furniture
☐ Masking tape
☐ Old rags to wipe up paint splashes

☐ Clean stick for stirring paint
☐ Roller tray
☐ Paint pad tray (optional)
☐ Paint kettle (optional)
☐ Extension handle for ceilings
  (eg broom handle)
☐ Working platform (eg 2 stepladders
  and plank of wood)

Extras for sponging:
☐ Natural sea sponge (hand-size)
☐ Shallow dish and spoon
☐ Waste paper (eg old wallpaper)

WHAT ABOUT TOOLS?

Most paints can be applied with a roller, brush or paint pad.

For emulsion, a roller is probably the most useful tool for covering large areas such as walls and ceilings quickly. You will, however, still need a brush or paint pad for smaller areas and awkward corners.

Rollers Buy a good quality lambswool or mohair roller (cheaper foam gives a poor finish) with a pile to suit the job – short pile for smooth surfaces, a longer pile for textured surfaces such as relief wallpapers.

There are special rollers with long handles for ceilings but with most standard rollers you can fit an extension (a broom handle is ideal) into the end of the handle.

Brushes These give good results but are slower than rollers. A 100mm wall brush is the best size for painting very large areas and a 25mm brush for filling in edges. Before using a new brush, wash it in warm water and tease out any loose bristles.

Paint pads These are light to use and won't splash but can be tricky to load with paint. Use a 225 × 100mm pad for large areas. An edging pad is useful for painting between walls and ceilings.

Paint tray You will need a special tray for loading a roller with paint (solid emulsion comes packed in its own tray). Paint trays are supplied with some paint pads but a roller tray or a deep can lid will do just as well.

Paint kettle If you're using a brush, a paint kettle (or any shallow, wide-topped container with a handle) is useful for decanting small quantities of paint. It's much easier to work with than a heavy paint tin, particularly if you're up a ladder.

Stepladders To reach ceilings and tops of walls, ideally you should rig up a working platform. A plank of wood wedged securely between two stepladders is safer than using a chair which can easily tip over.

Odds and ends Use masking tape (low-tack adhesive tape) for protecting light fittings, and have plenty of old rags for mopping and cleaning up.

Cleaning tools For cleaning off emulsion you need plenty of water. Emulsion dries fast, so wash your tools as soon as you have finished with them; get rid of excess paint on newspaper before rinsing thoroughly.

Hang brushes up with the bristles loosely held in shape with a rubber band; store flat when dry.

For short breaks – between coats, for instance – keep your tools from drying out by wrapping them in clingfilm or in a plastic bag sealed with an elastic band.

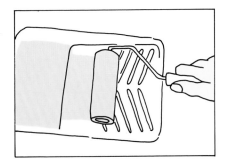

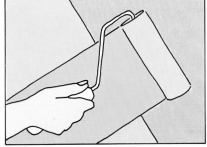

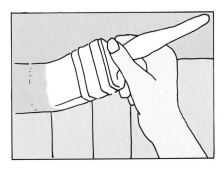

USING A ROLLER △
(Suitable for emulsion paints)
Pour some paint into the deep end of the roller tray, leaving the ridged section uncovered. Then dip the roller in the paint and run it back and forth over the ridged slope of the tray to distribute the paint evenly.

Roll the paint on to the wall with criss-cross diagonal strokes to cover a block. Start a second block alongside, avoiding ridges of excess paint by using a thinly-coated roller on overlaps. When painting ceilings wear goggles and a scarf for protection and don't let the roller spin freely or it will splash.

USING A BRUSH △
(Suitable for all types of paint)
Before using a new brush, wash it in warm water and tease out any loose bristles. Pour some paint into a paint kettle if you are using one. Load the brush by dipping just one-third of the bristles into the paint – don't overload the brush or paint may run back over the handle.

Apply paint using vertical strokes first, then change direction to spread paint evenly. Don't apply too much paint where blocks overlap.

USING A PAINT PAD ▷
(Suitable for emulsion paints)
Pour some paint into a paint tray and thin it with a little water. Hold the pad flat and dip only the mohair pile (never the foam backing) into the paint. Then draw the pad over the edge of the tray to wipe off any excess paint. Apply paint by lightly wiping the pad up and down over the wall surface.

ORDER OF PAINTING ▷

Paint the ceiling first, then the walls. Always start at the window end of a room and work away from the light as shown in the diagrams opposite – this makes it easier to see which areas have been painted.

Try to paint a ceiling, or a complete wall, in one burst – if you take a break in the middle, the dried edge may show as a definite mark when you have finished.

1 *Prepare to paint*
Wipe the lid of the paint tin clean of dust before opening it. Then stir the paint thoroughly with a clean wooden stick to shift any thick paint from the bottom. Do not stir non-drip gel paint.

2 *Paint ceiling edges and corners ▷*
First paint a narrow margin around the edges and corners of the ceiling using a narrow brush or edging pad.

To use an edging pad press its guide wheels against the wall ceiling junction and roll the pad along to get a sharp clean line. Don't overload the pad and make sure the wheels are paint free.

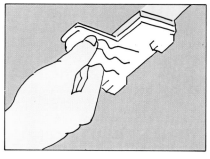

3 *Fill in the main ceiling area ▷*
Start in a corner at the window end of the room and work in manageable strips (about 1m wide) across the ceiling.

Ideally work from a platform (see checklist), a stepladder, or fit an extension handle to a roller so that you can paint the ceiling from the floor.

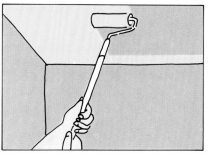

BRIGHT IDEA

Catch the drips If you're painting the ceiling with a brush, poke the handle through a foil dish or paper plate to catch the drips.

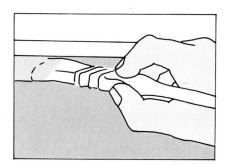

4 *Paint around features △*
Paint along the edges of skirtings, around window frames, light switches, etc, before you start to paint the main wall area. Use a small paint pad or a narrow brush (held edgeways on as shown).

Using an oil-based paint on walls ▷
Oil-based paint needs careful application (it's stickier and slower drying than emulsion) and you will get best results by using a brush. (Rollers and pads tend to leave marks.)

Apply the paint using criss-cross strokes as for emulsion, but finish off each section with light upward strokes to smooth out brush marks. Brush marks will show if you overlap dry paint so it's important to keep a wet edge around blocks.

Store brushes for short periods between painting by immersing just the bristles in water; shake out the water before using again.

When you have finished painting, clean your tools in white spirit or proprietary paintbrush cleaner, then wash in warm soapy water and rinse.

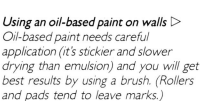

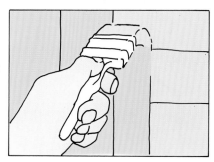

5 *Paint the walls*
Start at the top right-hand corner of a wall (top left if left-handed) and work across in horizontal bands from the ceiling downwards. This way you will be able to paint over any drips.

If small bubbles appear when painting over paper, leave them until the paint dries. Most will disappear but use a sharp razor blade to slit any that remain with a cross. Dab some wallpaper paste behind and flatten the paper. Retouch with paint when the area is completely dry.

SPONGING

Sponging is fun and fast to do, using matt or silk finish emulsion paints. By simply sponging on one or more toning or contrasting colours over a plain painted base you can create a pretty 'speckled egg' effect on your walls. A bright or pastel colour over white, for example, looks crisp and fresh, a light and dark tone of the same colour gives a more subtle effect – or try several colours such as pink, peach and cream over a yellow base. The results are infinitely variable, depending on the number of colours and the size and spacing of your sponge marks.

Use paint straight from the tin for strong prints, or dilute it with a little water to make softer marks.

Materials The only special equipment you need is a natural sea sponge of a size that fits comfortably in your hand.

You will also need a shallow dish for moistening the sponge with paint, and a spoon for transferring paint from the tin. Have plenty of scrap paper handy for testing prints (the back of left-over pieces of lining paper or wallpaper is ideal), and plenty of old rags for wiping up.

1 *Apply the base colour*
Paint the walls with the base colour and allow it to dry for at least 24 hours.

2 *Using the sponge △*
First, wet the sponge then wring it out so that it's just damp. Spoon about a tablespoon of the sponging colour into the shallow dish. Then either dip the flat side of the sponge into the paint or brush colour evenly on to the sponge with a paint brush.

Two-tone sponging ▽
Slightly denser sponging below the dado rail contrasts with the lighter stipple above it. Even the picture frames are decorated with this attractive finish.

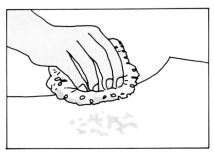

3 *Test the print △*
Gently pat the sponge on to the scrap paper. Splodgy wet prints mean that the sponge is overloaded with paint – keep dabbing until it leaves a soft, speckled mark.

4 *Sponge the wall △*
Starting at a corner, lightly dab sponge prints over the wall – turning the sponge round every so often to vary the mark it makes. Use a small piece of sponge to get into corners and a damp cloth to wipe off any smudges.

When the print gets faint, recharge the sponge with paint but always test the print first on paper. If the sponge gets clogged up, wipe it clean on rags or rinse in water.

5 *Sponge on two or more colours △*
If you're using several colours, space your first prints so that a good bit of base colour shows through. When the first sponged colour is dry, apply the second colour – then more if you wish. Fill gaps, but overlap prints too so that colours mingle.

6 *Check the finish*
Stand back now and then to judge the effect. If you've sponged on too much paint in places, it can be lightened once the paint is dry by sponging on a little base colour.

PREPARING AND PAINTING WOODWORK

Painting woodwork is not difficult but these surfaces get a lot of hard wear so good preparation is a must.

Bright, freshly painted woodwork — from windows and doors to staircases and skirtings — adds greatly to the appearance of a newly decorated room.

This chapter covers preparing and painting woodwork with oil-based paints. Carefully applied, these paints give a durable finish that is easy to keep clean.

Check the wood is sound If wood is riddled with rot, there's no point in redecorating. Unsound wood is usually warped and has a broken surface. Stick a sharp pointed tool (a small screwdriver will do) into any suspect areas — if the blade goes in easily in several places, call in a specialist to investigate.

Preparing woodwork Old paintwork that is sound only needs washing down, and a little filling and sanding to hide small cracks and nail holes. Only strip paint if it is peeling or blistering badly, or if there is a thick build-up of old paint.

New wood needs to be sanded smooth, and knots sealed with knotting compound to stop resin bleeding through subsequent layers of paint.

When to paint woodwork Prepare the woodwork at the same time as any other surfaces to be decorated. Paint the woodwork after you've done the walls and ceiling, but before you lay new flooring.

Paint windows first, then any cupboards or shelves, then doors, and finally the skirting.

WHICH PAINT?

Full-gloss paint gives the toughest finish but shows up imperfections. If the surface is a bit rough, an eggshell finish — halfway between gloss and matt — may be preferable.

Starting from scratch New wood requires a wood primer first, then an

Neat paintwork
Gloss paint, carefully applied, enhances the attractive woodwork in this traditional entrance hall.

undercoat in a colour to suit the topcoat. With non-drip gloss and eggshell paints undercoat is not always necessary.

Painting existing paintwork One topcoat is usually enough but, if you're painting a light colour over a dark one, you may need undercoat and two topcoats to get a good finish. (See Interior Paints for suitable types of paints.)

HOW MUCH PAINT?

Covering capacity varies from one paint brand to the next – as a rough guide, a door takes about 1/10 of a litre for each coat.

TOOLS AND EQUIPMENT

Abrasive paper to smooth surfaces and provide a key for new paint. Use glasspaper on new wood. For rubbing down existing paintwork, wet-and-dry paper is useful as it can be rinsed clean when it becomes clogged with paint. You will need fine, medium and coarse-grade paper.

A sanding block Wrap abrasive paper round a block of wood or cork when sanding a flat surface. For mouldings, wrap paper round a sponge instead.

A scraper to remove loose or blistering paint.

Ready-mixed fine surface filler to cover surface dents and small holes.

Interior-grade cellulose filler to fill cracks and holes deeper than 2mm or open joints (eg, between skirting and the wall). It comes as powder to be mixed with water.

Paint brushes A 50 or 75mm brush for large areas; a 25mm brush for panels and skirting. A 19mm cutting-in brush with angled bristles is useful for painting straight lines, up to corners and awkward edges.

Masking tape for protecting surfaces when painting straight lines.

A shield is useful when painting up to edges – use a piece of stiff cardboard, or buy a special plastic or metal paint shield.

CHECK YOUR NEEDS

☐ Oil-based paint
☐ Primer (on new or bare wood)
☐ Undercoat (optional)
☐ 50 or 75mm paintbrush
☐ 25mm paintbrush
☐ 19mm cutting-in brush
☐ Masking tape, paint shield
☐ White spirit or paint brush cleaner/restorer
☐ Dust sheets and newspaper for protecting surfaces
☐ Cleaning up rags

Preparation details:
☐ Sugar soap or household detergent
☐ Plastic bucket
☐ Sponge or cloth
☐ Rubber gloves
☐ Abrasive paper
☐ Sanding block
☐ Scraper
☐ All-purpose cellulose filler
☐ Filling knife (or old table knife)
☐ Knotting compound, hair dryer

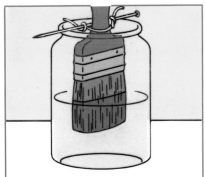

TAKING CARE OF PAINT BRUSHES

Before using a new brush, wash it in warm water and tease out any loose bristles.

After use, wipe excess paint on newspaper, then clean the brush in white spirit or paint brush cleaner. Wash in warm soapy water and rinse well.

Soak an old, hardened brush in paint brush cleaner before washing – if bristles remain stuck together, throw it away.

Store brushes during breaks by immersing just the bristles in water; shake out the water before using again. To stop bristles being bent out of shape, use a nail and string to suspend the brush over a jar.

1 Wash old paintwork
Wash down paintwork with a sponge and solution of warm water and sugar soap or household detergent to remove dirt and grease. Rinse with clean water and leave to dry.

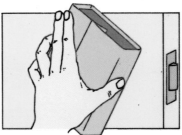

2 Sand down △
Sand old paintwork lightly along the grain to remove the shine and provide a key for new paint. Use fine-grade wet-and-dry paper wrapped round a sanding block, and sprinkled with soapy water. Rinse paper clean from time to time in water.

Dust off, then wipe over paintwork with a cloth dipped in white spirit and leave to dry.

New wood Sand down along the grain of the wood with medium then fine-grade glasspaper, and round off sharp edges. Remove surface dust with a cloth dampened with white spirit.

3 Remove loose paint
Remove small areas of loose or blistered paint with a scraper, keeping the blade as flat to the surface as possible. Take back to bare wood if necessary, and rub down the edges of the stripped patch with coarse-grade glasspaper until flush.

4 Fill dents, holes and joints
Fill nicks and dents with fine surface filler; fill larger holes with interior-grade cellulose filler. Dab oil-based paint on to nail and screw heads before covering.

Apply filler with a filling knife or an old table knife and level off by drawing the blade across the surface. When dry, rub smooth with fine-grade glasspaper.

For awkward gaps, pack filler in with your finger (wearing a rubber glove) and wipe over immediately with a damp rag to smooth the surface.

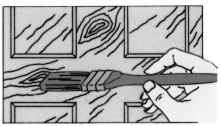

5 Seal knots in bare wood △
If there are lots of knots in bare wood, heat each knot with a hair dryer to draw out the resin. Let this dry, then scrape away the resin and seal the knot by painting on two thin coats of knotting compound.

6 *Apply primer/undercoat*
First, prime new wood (and any bare or filled patches in a painted surface) with a thin coat of primer. Leave to dry thoroughly, then gently rub smooth with fine-grade glasspaper.

After priming, apply undercoat if you are using liquid gloss paint or if you are changing the existing colour radically. Brush on one coat and leave to dry.

7 *Prepare to paint* ▷
Wipe the lid of the paint tin clean of dust before removing it. If stirring the paint is recommended (check on the tin), use a clean wooden stick in a figure-of-eight motion to shift pigment from the bottom of the tin. DO NOT STIR NON-DRIP GLOSS.

If a thick skin has formed on paint already opened, cut round the outside of it with a sharp knife and remove it in one piece if possible before stirring. When you

load your brush, dip just one-third of the bristles into the paint. Avoid getting paint in the metal ferrule of the handle or it may drip.

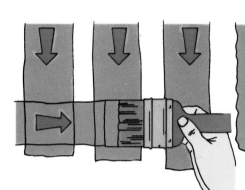
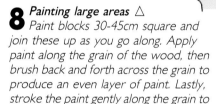

8 *Painting large areas* △
Paint blocks 30-45cm square and join these up as you go along. Apply paint along the grain of the wood, then brush back and forth across the grain to produce an even layer of paint. Lastly, stroke the paint gently along the grain to get a smooth finish.

Keep paint thin where blocks overlap to avoid ridges forming, and always work against a 'wet' block so that you can blend in the fresh paint.

To prevent a build-up of paint on the edge of a door, for example, always brush out towards the edge – not in from it.

KEEP THE EDGE OF THE TIN CLEAN
To prevent dribbles and build up of paint round the rim, tape or tie a length of string across the top of the tin and use this to remove excess paint from the brush. Alternatively, you can buy a special plastic ring to fit on to the top of a 1 litre tin.

9 *Painting small areas*
Use a 25mm brush to apply paint in a series of dabs about 6cm apart, then join them up.

Cover narrow sections, such as glazing bars of windows, by simply stroking the paint along the grain of the wood.

10 *Painting straight edges* △
When painting along edges such as skirting boards or window frames, protect the floor or glass with masking tape. Peel it off glass as soon as the paint is dry – otherwise it is difficult to remove.

Alternatively, protect the surface by holding a piece of stiff cardboard or a paint shield. Wipe it clean of paint each time it's moved to a new position.

Cutting in Where you can't or don't want to use tape or a shield, use a cutting-in brush with angled bristles to paint a straight edge, or adapt an ordinary narrow brush.

Load the brush lightly and hold it as shown – rather like a pencil. Slowly push it in to meet the join, then press lightly and draw it along firmly to make a straight line.

BRIGHT IDEA

PAINT A SHARP EDGE
Adapt an ordinary narrow brush for cutting in (or make an angled brush even more effective) by wrapping an elastic band around the bristles to stop them splaying out too much.

ORDER OF PAINTING: WINDOWS

Unscrew all fastenings, and open the window when painting.

When painting the rebates (where wood and glass meet), run a thin line of paint on to the glass to seal the putty. Any paint smudges can be scraped off when dry with a razor blade; use nail polish remover to take off paint on reeded glass.

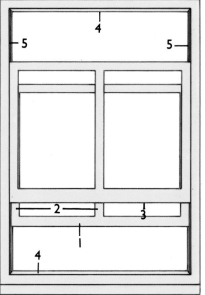

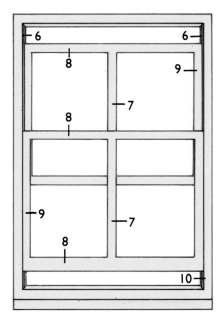

Casement windows △

Begin with **1** the inside edge of the frame and **2** the opening edge of the window. Then paint **3** all the rebates, **4** the glazing bars, **5-6** the top and bottom horizontal rails, **7** the hinged stile, **8** the meeting stile, and lastly, **9** the window frame and sill.

Do not close the window until the paint is completely dry.

Sash windows △

Raise the bottom sash and pull the top sash down, so that you can paint **1** the meeting rail (including its rebate and bottom edge).

Then paint as much as you can of **2** the glazing bars (including the rebates) and stiles on the upper sash, **3** the bottom edge of the lower sash, **4** the inside edge of the frame, and **5** a short way down the outside runners.

Leave paint to dry, then reposition the window as shown (closing it almost completely) and paint **6** what you can of the inside runners. Then paint **7** all the rebates and glazing bars, **8** the remaining cross rails, and **9** the stiles. Lastly paint **10** the window frame, architrave and sill.

Make sure you do not paint the sash cords.

ORDER OF PAINTING: DOORS

Unscrew and remove all fittings apart from the hinges. Wedge the door open with a block of wood, and slide a bin bag or newspaper underneath to protect the floor.

Paint the edges of a flush or panel door before you paint the face of it or the frame. With the door opening towards you, paint the opening edge; with it opening away, paint the hinged edge. Unless you can see a door from above, there's no need to paint the top of it.

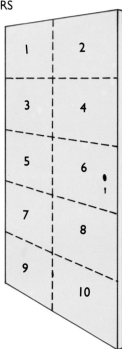

Flush doors ◁

Paint a flat door in sections about 40cm square using a 75mm brush. Start at the top and work quickly across the door, then down it in bands. Paint the door frame and architrave last, and leave the door ajar until dry.

Panel doors ▷

Begin with the inset panels **1-4**, painting each panel immediately after its moulding.

Next paint the central vertical section **5-6**, then the horizontal sections **7-9** (top bar, middle bar, then the bottom one). Then paint the outer vertical sections **10-11**.

Lastly, paint the door frame and architrave.

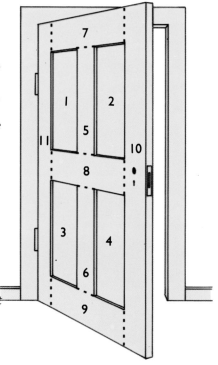

SPECIAL EFFECTS WITH PAINT

Ragging, rag-rolling or stippling:
these paint techniques create
a wonderful variety of effects, and
they're fun and easy to do.

A broken colour finish is an exciting alternative to plainly painted walls, and most will actually help to disguise any minor imperfections in the surface.

Ragging, rag-rolling and stippling all involve painting a top 'glaze' coat over a lighter base coat, then breaking up the wet glaze in some way to give depth and texture to the surface.

The techniques are straightforward, but you do have to work fast: on large surfaces such as walls it's best if two people work together.

Ragging and rag-rolling produce a bold, rich texture like crushed velvet, using bunched-up rags that are pressed into or rolled over the wet glaze. It looks good on a large scale, and is quite quick to do.

You'll need a large supply of rags as they soon get soaked with paint. Old sheets make good lint-free rags; for different effects try well-washed hessian, cheesecloth, paper, or even plastic bags.

Stippling gives a very subtle, fine-textured finish with a soft-bristled brush used to lift off just enough colour for the background to show through. Time consuming and fairly tiring on a large scale, it looks good on woodwork and furniture as well as walls: the method is the same.

For best results you can buy special stippling brushes made of fine bristle, but these are very expensive. You can improvise fairly successfully with a painter's dusting brush, or a soft-bristled broom or old clothes brush as long as it has a blunt, level surface.

Colour schemes Although the tone of the top glaze coat is the dominating one, the colour you choose for the base coat influences the finished effect. A white base gives soft, glowing colour; for a richer look, try a pastel-coloured base and pick a darker tone for the glaze. With ragging or rag-rolling, you can achieve subtle effects by using two slightly different but harmonious colours on top of each other.

Whichever finish you choose, experiment with different colour schemes and practise the technique on pre-painted board or card until you feel happy with the effect. The more you practise, the better the results.

PREPARATION

Surfaces to be painted should be clean and sound. Although slightly bumpy walls are less obvious with a ragged or stippled finish, the ideal surface is smooth and even.

For basic preparation tasks, see Preparing Walls, pages 7-10; walls that are very shabby but otherwise sound are best covered with lining paper, see Hanging Wallpaper, pages 61-64.

Then paint on the base coat and leave to dry thoroughly, allowing up to 24 hours before applying the glaze coat.

Ragged looks ▽
This finish – using a warm terracotta base, ragged with a transparent burnt sienna – makes a striking background for deep mahogany bedroom furniture.

WHICH PAINT?

The base coat One or two coats of eggshell oil-based paint is ideal: the result is a smooth, non-absorbent base over which the glaze slides easily and doesn't sink in. Eggshell doesn't normally need undercoat, but prime any bare surfaces.

Vinyl silk emulsion is a reasonable substitute and, being water-based, it's easier to apply. You'll probably need to apply two coats of vinyl silk for good coverage.

The glaze coat The traditional glaze is semi-transparent – based on a transparent oil glaze (or scumble glaze) that is tinted to the right colour and thinned with white spirit to a workable consistency. It dries slowly, so that you have enough time to work on the finish, and holds the decorative patterns distinctly.

Depending on the brand, transparent oil glaze ranges from off-white to a deep gold colour when looked at in the tin. When brushed out it goes transparent but does tend to yellow slightly with age. Available from specialist paint shops; about half a litre glazes a small room.

Tinting Transparent oil glaze can be tinted with universal stainers, which are cheap, strong and come in basic colours, or artists' oil colours, which are more expensive but are available in a huge range of shades. Universal stainers are sold by most DIY shops; artists' oils by art shops.

For light shades, mix the tinting colours into a base of white eggshell paint. This makes the glaze more opaque, and softens the effect of the decorative finish.

WAYS OF WORKING

On large surfaces such as walls, these finishes are easier and much less tiring if two people work together.

One person applies a strip of glaze, the other follows closely behind and starts treating it before it dries; meanwhile, the first painter begins applying another strip of glaze. The trick is to keep out of each other's way but with a little practise you'll soon get a good, speedy rhythm going. – essential for a successful finish.

It's a good idea to start off on a window wall where any beginner's mistakes will be less noticeable.

Always paint at least a whole wall in one session, stopping if necessary at a corner. If you stop in the middle of a wall, the dried edge may show as a definite join when you've finished.

CHECK YOUR NEEDS

For the base coat:
- ☐ Oil-based eggshell paint (prime bare surfaces first)
- ☐ 100mm paint brush

For the glaze coat:
- ☐ Transparent oil glaze
- ☐ White spirit
- ☐ White plastic paint kettle

For tinting the glaze:
- ☐ Universal stainer/artists' oil colour
- ☐ White oil-based paint (for light colours)
- ☐ Saucer or bowl
- ☐ Narrow long-handled paint brush for mixing
- ☐ Old spoon
- ☐ Scrap paper for testing

For the finish:
- ☐ 100mm paint brush for applying glaze
- ☐ White cotton rags, about 40cm square, for ragging/rag rolling
  OR
  Stippling brush (or painter's dusting brush, soft-bristled broom or clothes brush)
- ☐ Stepladder for tops of walls
- ☐ Plastic sheets/newspaper
- ☐ Rags for mopping up
- ☐ Rubber gloves

SAFETY

Rags soaked in paint and solvent are highly inflammable: let them dry out completely before disposing of them carefully.

1 Tint the glaze △

Tinting glaze to exactly the right shade is a matter of experimenting so use small amounts of tints – artists' oil colours or universal stainers – at a time (a couple of inches squeezed from the tube is plenty). Aim to mix enough glaze for the whole room, but keep a note of the formula so you can remix if necessary.

Squeeze the colours into a saucer, add just enough white spirit to wet the colour and dissolve it, and blend with a paint brush. (For light colour, add the dissolved tints to white oil-based paint – 10-20% paint to 80-90% glaze). Then spoon in a little transparent oil glaze, stir until colour is evenly dispersed, and test on thick white paper. Bear in mind that the tone lightens when you add the rest of the glaze and white spirit, and appears less intense when brushed out sparingly on a wall.

When you're satisfied with the colour mix it up with the remainder of the glaze in a paint kettle; stir well.
Test by brushing glaze very thinly over white paper and leave to dry – it looks softer as it dries.

2 Thin the glaze ▽

Use white spirit to dilute tinted glaze to a workable consistency. As the different glazes vary in thickness, start with 1 part white spirit to 2 parts glaze increasing the white spirit gradually (up to 2 parts), testing as you go. The more white spirit you add the quicker the glaze dries.

Test the glaze on a pre-painted board or a small area of wall (you can wipe it off with a rag dampened with white spirit). Keep the glaze to a thin film or it may run and apply quickly and lightly with a wide paint brush.

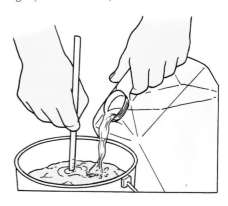

STIPPLING

Lifting off tiny flecks of wet glaze with a stippling brush gives a very finely speckled colour: the effect is soft and unobtrusive.

1 *Apply the glaze*
Use an ordinary wide paint brush to apply a thin film of glaze as evenly as possible.

Starting in one corner of the room, cover the wall from top to bottom with a strip of glaze about 30-60cm wide – whatever seems most manageable. Don't cover too large an area at one time or the paint will dry before you can stipple the surface.

2 *Stipple the glaze* △
Use a stippling brush or suitable soft-bristled brush held at right angles to the surface, to break up the colour. Stab the tips of the bristles gently but firmly into the wet glaze – do not skid over the surface. Work over the strip of wet glaze leaving a narrow band on the outer edge unstippled.

Remove build-up of glaze from the brush frequently by brushing it out on paper. If necessary, wipe the bristles clean with white spirit.

3 *Repeat the technique*
Apply another strip of glaze so that it slightly overlaps with the first, then stipple the wet glaze as before.

Check the finish Stand back every so often to judge the effect. If you've left too much paint on some patches, try dabbing with the cleaned stippling brush. If the glaze is too dry to stipple, moisten the area with a rag dampened with white spirit, then use a clean stippling brush.

RAGGING

Ragging creates a bold crushed velvet look. Rag-rolling (below) is similar but the effect is more directional.

1 Prepare the rag
Soak a lint-free rag in white spirit, squeeze out and dry by squeezing in a fresh rag. This prevents the rag clogging with paint too quickly.

2 Apply the glaze
Starting in one corner of the room, brush on a thin even film of glaze to cover a strip of wall 30-60cm wide from top to bottom. The glaze need not be brushed out absolutely smooth, but should cover the base colour well so that the rag prints show up clearly.

3 Rag the glaze ▷
Bunch the rag up into a loose wedge. Then press it lightly and quickly over the wet glaze, slightly overlapping the prints to get a distinct but soft, crinkled finish.
Keep changing the direction of your hand as you work and refold the rag every so often to avoid repetition. You can rinse the rag clean in white spirit, but change it for a fresh one when it gets clogged with glaze.

4 Repeat the technique
Brush glaze on to the next strip of wall, overlapping the first strip just a little so that you don't get a build up of colour along the join. Then rag the wet glaze. Continue painting and ragging the wall a section at a time.
A second ragged colour can be applied once the first coat has dried thoroughly (it takes about a week).

Check the finish Stand back every now and then to judge your work. If you've missed a patch, touch it in lightly with a glaze-wet rag. If there's a patch with too much glaze, rub off with a rag dampened with white spirit and immediately glaze and rag over again, blending it into the first glaze coat.

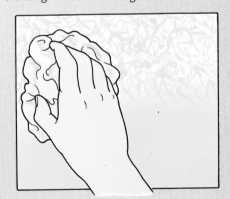

RAG-ROLLING

Apply the glaze in the same way as for ragging, but bunch the rag into a small sausage shape. Then lightly roll the rag up the wall (or down it, if that's easier) in an irregular, meandering line from bottom to top. One roll-up (or roll down) should only just overlap with the next to prevent taking off too much glaze. Take care not to skid over the surface as you roll.
Leave a narrow band on the outer edge untouched to avoid brushing new glaze into an already ragged pattern. You can blend in the join when you rag-roll the next section. Replace rag with a new one as soon as it is saturated with glaze.

COLOUR WASHING AND SHADING

Give your walls an added depth of colour and a soft finish with one of these special paint effects.

Colour washing and shading are the plainest paint techniques used by the professional decorator. They are relatively easy to apply (washing is easier than shading), giving broad brush effects which are very different from the more defined markings achieved by sponging or ragging.

Colour washing has an informal cottagey look. Use thinned emulsion paint over an emulsion base for the appeal of old-fashioned distemper without its drawbacks. (Distemper was not a washable finish, and had to be removed before re-decoration. It also tended to come off if you rubbed against the wall.) The base coat should be white, or near white, with a darker colour washed over it. For a more sophisticated finish, use eggshell paint for the base, and wash over an oil-based glaze to give more of a sheen. Again, the glaze is tinted to a darker shade than the base coat.

The technique in each case is the same: the wall is given a base coat of emulsion or eggshell paint, and two thinned topcoats (of water-based paint over emulsion or oil based paint over eggshell) are brushed over randomly.

Colour shading is a more precise technique. Bands of coloured glaze are applied to a base coat and then carefully stippled to get a gently graduated effect. It's usual to start with the deepest colour at skirting level and to finish with the palest tint or tone when you reach the ceiling, giving the room an open, airy feeling. However, you can reverse the process if you want to reduce the room's apparent height.

You can also give emphasis to the centre of a wall by shading it from light in the centre to darker shades at the edges. Colour shading is also a popular technique for decorating panelled doors round the house, on cupboards and kitchen units.

CHOOSING COLOURS

Because the aim of colour washing is to create a mellow, 'distressed' or artificially worn effect, it's best to choose soft colours and pastels, giving an impression that stronger shades have been used and have faded. Think of apricot, aquamarine, apple green, butter yellow or old rose for walls — tones which reflect the gentle colours of nature.

Apply the top coat on a white base for a translucent effect, or over a paler version of the same colour for richness.

If you are colour shading you can use stronger colours, though it's wise not to have too wide a variation in tone or shade in a small room. If you are shading the walls in different tones of the same colour, a look at the paint manufacturers' charts for specially mixed paints will give you some ideas. These ranges add different amounts of tint to a few base colours to produce related tones in different strengths. For colour shading with two different shades, it is important to choose two colours which will blend together well — coffee to cream, blue to lilac and so on.

The gentle touch
Bring a softness to plain walls with a wash of apricot over a cream background. The added warmth gives a welcoming touch to an otherwise formal room. The nearly plain walls show off the fireplace and pictures perfectly.

PREPARATION

For any kind of painted finish, you should always prepare walls carefully – particularly if you intend to use a paint with a sheen finish like eggshell which highlights every bump. However, one of the joys of a rustic technique like colour washing is that the surface does not have to be totally flat.

Colour shading requires more attention, and it is particularly important that your base coat is even, so that porous patches in your walls don't absorb the bands of tint unevenly, creating darker patches.

Always remove old wallpaper before attempting either of these techniques, fill cracks and sand them level in the usual way (see Preparing Walls). Hang lining paper if necessary.

If you are re-decorating walls finished with an oil-based finish, for example eggshell or gloss, sand them lightly to provide a key for the next coat. Wash and rinse all painted walls.

If the walls are flaky, scrape flaking paint well. Finish with a coat of stabilizing primer to get an evenly porous surface. Also, use stabilizing primer if you have had to wash away distemper.

TOOLS AND EQUIPMENT

Colour washing Besides paint, brushes and roller or pads for applying the base coat, the only tools and materials you will need are a wide wall paint brush (100mm), a paint kettle and the glaze or wash itself. For matt colour washing you will need emulsion paint thinned with water, and for an eggshell glaze you will need to mix the glaze from 50 per cent eggshell paint, 20 per cent white spirit and 30 per cent oil glaze (see Special Effects with Paint). (For a more translucent finish, use a mix of 30 per cent eggshell paint, 30 per cent white spirit, 30 per cent glaze and 10 per cent matt finish clear varnish.)

Colour shading For colour shading, you need to mix several batches of paint (four or five), so use several paint kettles and empty jars to mix your glaze. The glaze should be made from 70 per cent oil glaze, 20 per cent eggshell, 10 per cent white spirit. The tones or shades of paint are mixed first. To shade from dark to light, add increasing amounts of white eggshell.

You will also need a paint roller and tray for applying the shades, and a stippling brush to blur the edges.

MIXING A COLOUR WASH

Using emulsion Tip some emulsion paint into a paint kettle and thin with water following the manufacturer's directions on the back of the tin (the normal proportions are 1 part water to 4 parts of paint) and stir well.

Using a glaze Although the glaze used for colour washing is thinner than the normal 'recipe' used for colour shading and decorative paint techniques such as rag-rolling and stippling, the method used for making the glaze is the same – simply mix the paint and oil glaze, stir well with a clean stick, then add the appropriate amount of white spirit to thin the glaze sufficiently and make it easy to work.

CHECK YOUR NEEDS
For the base coat:
- ☐ Paint for base coat (emulsion or eggshell)
- ☐ Brush for cutting in
- ☐ Roller and paint tray
- ☐ Washing up liquid and warm water for cleaning brushes and rollers after using emulsion, or white spirit for cleaning after using eggshell paint (and oil-based glaze)

For colour washing:
- ☐ A glaze of 50 per cent eggshell, 20 per cent white spirit and 30 per cent oil glaze (for use over eggshell paint, see above)

OR
- ☐ Thinned emulsion paint (for use over an emulsion base)
- ☐ 100mm wall brush
- ☐ Paint kettle

For colour shading:
- ☐ Several batches of glaze made up from 70 per cent oil glaze, 20 per cent eggshell paint and 10 per cent white spirit
- ☐ Empty jars to mix colours
- ☐ Paint kettles to mix glaze
- ☐ Roller and tray
- ☐ Stippling brush
- ☐ White spirit and plenty of rags

COLOUR WASHING ON WALLS

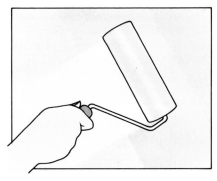

1 Applying the base coat △
Apply one or two base coats of white or lightly coloured paint (you can use either emulsion or eggshell) leaving to dry between coats if you are applying more than one coat. Because the walls don't need to be perfectly evenly coloured, one coat of paint should be sufficient in most cases. Work the paint carefully in all directions using diagonal strokes as shown.

2 Applying the first wash △
Dip the wall brush in the thinned emulsion or mixed glaze and paint the wall with random movements, working quickly to prevent drips and runs. If drips and runs start to form, work them in quickly before they begin to dry. Leave some of the background uncovered but take care to soften any hard lines. Leave emulsion to dry for four hours, glaze for at least 12 hours.

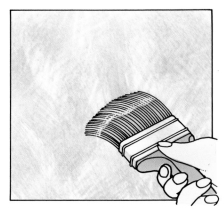

3 Applying the second wash △
Repeat the step over the previous wash to cover the base coat again. Leave to dry as before.

4 Protective finish
If you want a hard-wearing surface, finish with a coat of matt or silk polyurethane varnish (add a dash of white eggshell paint to prevent yellowing).

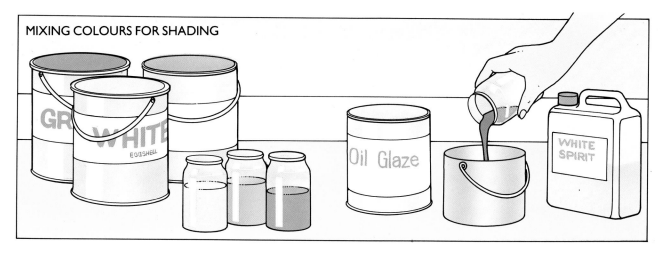

MIXING COLOURS FOR SHADING

1 Mixing the colours △
Start by mixing two shades of eggshell paint to give the desired number of shades. It's a good idea to use empty jam jars or coffee jars, so you can see the colours clearly and check that they are thoroughly mixed. The four or five shades which you mix should be evenly graded. You can also use coloured and white eggshell paint.

2 Mixing the glaze △
In the paint kettles, mix the oil glaze and white spirit, ensuring that all the mixtures are in exactly the same proportions. Then add the mixed paint to the glaze to give the mixture 70 per cent oil glaze, 20 per cent paint and 10 per cent white spirit. Stir thoroughly to ensure all the ingredients are evenly mixed.

Note: the more white spirit you add the quicker the paint will dry, so stick to the 'recipe' as the bands of colour will be more difficult to blend if the paint dries too quickly.

COLOUR SHADING ON WALLS

1 Applying the base coat
Apply one or two coats of eggshell paint in the palest shade as a base coat, allowing plenty of time for the paint to dry (see manufacturer's instructions on side of tin). It is essential to get an even finish, so in most cases both coats will be needed.

2 Mark the bands
Decide how wide the bands of colour should be. The width depends on the height of the wall and the number of colours. For example, on a 3000mm wall, with four shading colours, each band will be 750mm wide. Use a pencil to mark a very light line right across the wall between each of the bands of colour, to give you a guide to the width of the bands when you come to apply the colours.

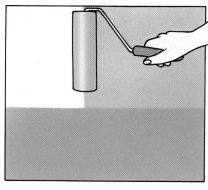

3 Applying the first band △
Tip the darkest batch of glaze into the base of the roller tray and paint a horizontal band right along the wall above the skirting. (This is for walls shaded from dark to light, bottom to top. For other effects start with the darkest colour at the top of the wall, or round the edges of the wall, as appropriate.)

4 Applying the next band of colour △
Clean the roller and tray and tip the second colour into the tray. Apply a second band above the first, so that the edges meet. Apply the colours in quick succession, so the first coat does not have a chance to dry out.

5 Softening the effect ◁
With the stippling brush, stipple up and down each band, 'pouncing' the brush softly up and down to produce the desired effect. Wipe the brush regularly using clean, lint-free rags, to prevent a build-up of glaze on the bristles. Stipple carefully over the join between the two bands of colour to spread the colour and blur the edge where the two bands meet. Then clean the stippling brush between bands, using white spirit or brush cleanser.

6 Repeat the technique
Apply the next band and repeat until you reach the ceiling. It is important to work quickly and be relaxed when you work to get as smooth and even a finish as possible. Remember you can always go over the wall again if you are not totally satisfied with the result.

METHOD OF WORKING

It is easier to achieve a good effect if you work with a partner, one applying the paint and the other using the stippling brush. The first person applies the first band of paint, and after applying a couple of metres of the second band of paint, the second person can start stippling to blend the two bands.

If you prefer to apply the base coat with a brush, it is worth having a separate brush for each kettle of paint so that you don't have to wash out the brushes between colours.

BRIGHT IDEA

Crafty art Highlight a picture by shading from a darker shade around the edge of the wall to a lighter shade around the picture. For a completely co-ordinated effect, use card for the picture mount in a shade which exactly matches the darkest colour used for shading. You can either paint the other walls in the darker shade, or repeat the shading effect on them. For this effect, it is best to use tones of one colour (achieved by mixing different amounts of white into a colour) rather than using two colours.

◁ *Successful shades*
Both the walls and the woodwork in this room have been shaded in tones of blue and green to give a gently graduated effect. The overall effect is emphasized by the use of neutral tones for curtains, sofa and accessories.

SPECKLED PAINT EFFECTS

Spattering and cissing are both ways of creating a speckled paint finish. Spattering is the easier of the two.

More defined than stippling, more delicate than sponging, spattering and cissing are two techniques which are superficially similar. Both employ tiny spots of colour to produce a speckled look – the main difference is that cissing involves softening the effect with a solvent, and is best carried out on horizontal surfaces to avoid drips and runs.

Spattering requires little more than courage. No special brushes or paints are required (though you should use a purpose-made paint for spattering on china and glass and heat-set dyes for use on fabric). Nor need you have a fixed idea of the end result because spattering is one of the techniques that's best created in stages – simply choose your colours and step back to assess the result after applying each one.

What you do have to be careful to do is to mask the surrounding area thoroughly. If the piece is portable, spatter it in a workshop or garage, or outside on a still day. You'll also need to take care not to overload the brush, which would produce splodges and streaks rather than spots.

Cissing, on the other hand, is a highly sophisticated technique. Unlike spattering, which is a random finish, it mimics the striations of natural stone. (It's also known as fossilizing because this is the look it's supposed to convey.) Purists keep pebbles and pieces of rock by them as they work so that they can reproduce the appearance but cissing can also be carried out in pastel colours for a fantasy effect. In cissing, white spirit is used to remove colour and soften the design – a type of reverse spattering. Usually, a final, darker colour is spattered over the surface to add extra definition. There are four main steps involved in creating this finish so it's not one to rush.

COLOUR SENSE

Spattering looks particularly effective in contrasting colours, especially if these relate to the room scheme, and two shades of one colour is a sophisticated alternative. It's often used to co-ordinate accessories like china, trays or cushions, combining two or three of the room's predominant colours, and generally looks best on a white or a pale toning ground. Think of peach and blue on a pale apricot or white, for example; pink and green on pistachio or primrose yellow and lavender on lemon. But dramatic colour combinations like blue and purple on black, or orange on pink, can also look good.

Cissing is best done in softer colours. Blend the purple-pink of a crystalline rock like porphyry or the yellow-green of semi-precious stones like tourmaline or peridot with ivory and beige for a realistic effect and finish with polyurethane varnish, which brings out the colours like a rain-washed pebble.

All-over cover
Walls, woodwork and fire surround have all been spattered in tones of blue and white on a pale blue background. White ceramic ornaments and furnishings with simple lines complement, rather than compete with, the effect.

PREPARATION

Whatever the surface you are going to cover, it should be clean and smooth. Rub down gloss- or eggshell-painted surfaces with glass paper to provide a key, and prime bare wood before applying the base coat. Old wood may need renovation before you can embark on a decorative paint technique. Strip away existing paint or varnish using a proprietary stripper or hot air gun and fill cracks with wood filler. Sand along the grain to a fine finish, by hand for small pieces or with an orbital sander for large flat areas. Seal any knots with knotting solution to prevent resin bleeding out and wipe the wood clean with white spirit. Apply wood primer, then two base coats of eggshell paint.

China and glass must be clean and grease-free so wash, rinse and dry, then wipe over with white spirit.

It is possible to spatter walls if you take care to achieve a fine spray of paint so that the spots won't run. In this case simply prepare the surface in the usual way. Remember that the wall will be speckled rather than covered with paint, so the base coat must be even.

TOOLS AND EQUIPMENT

Spattering Choose paint to suit the object you are spattering: emulsion for walls; enamel or proprietary china paint for china and glass; gloss or enamel for metal and eggshell, gloss or lacquer for wood. In addition you will need white spirit for thinning all the paints except emulsion, also for brush cleaning, and clear polyurethane varnish to give the spattering a protective finish. Choose gloss or matt according to the effect you want to achieve. Paint brushes required are a 75mm or 100mm wall brush for large areas, a stiff artists' paint brush for small items and a separate new brush for applying varnish. Lastly you will need a straightedge or ruler on which to tap the brush when spattering.

Cissing The main requirement for cissing is the glaze. Make up three or four batches, using an equal mixture of scumble (oil glaze) and oil-based paint (see Special Effects with Paint). Choose colours which will blend together. Paint brushes required are two soft artists' brushes (say numbers 6 and 8) and a sword liner (or fine brush such as an eyeliner brush). In addition you will need a lint-free cloth with which to blend the first two or three glaze coats. You will also need a straightedge or ruler, white spirit, varnish and brush.

SPATTERING

1 *Apply the base coat*
After preparing the surface apply two base coats: eggshell or gloss paint on wood, emulsion or eggshell on walls. Leave until dry (16 hours for oil-based paint, four hours for emulsion).

2 *Experiment with the paint*
Thin eggshell or gloss paint with white spirit and emulsion with water if necessary to obtain a good consistency. Experiment by spattering on newspaper until you are satisfied with the result.

3 *Apply the spatter* ▷
Dip the brush into the paint so that no more than one third of the bristle length is covered. Lift it a short distance over or next to the item to be spattered and tap the base of the handle on the straightedge to create a fine shower of paint. Continue until you have covered the piece and allow to dry completely.
Repeat the process (far right) using a second colour and leave to dry again. Apply a third colour if required.

4 *Varnish the spatter* ▷
When the spattering is completely dry, cover it with a protective layer of varnish. One coat is sufficient for decorative pieces, but use three on items subject to a lot of wear, such as table tops. Add a trace of white eggshell or gloss to the varnish to stop it yellowing.

CHECK YOUR NEEDS

For spattering
- ☐ Oil- or water-based paint (to suit the surface)
- ☐ White spirit if required
- ☐ Large or small paint brush
- ☐ Straightedge or ruler
- ☐ Polyurethane varnish
- ☐ Varnish brush
- ☐ Old newspapers

For cissing
- ☐ Three or four batches of oil-based glaze
- ☐ Two artists' brushes
- ☐ Sword liner or fine brush
- ☐ Lint-free cloth
- ☐ White spirit
- ☐ Straightedge
- ☐ Polyurethane varnish
- ☐ Varnish brush or new paint brush

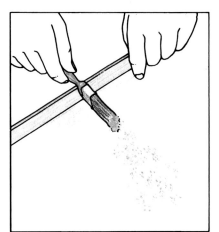

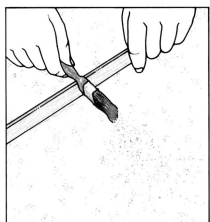

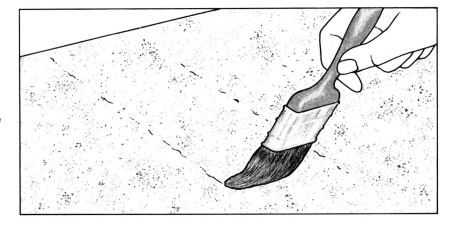

CISSING

Cissing involves dabbing two or three different glazes on a flat surface, merging the colours, spattering with white spirit and then spattering a final, darker coloured glaze on the surface.

Here we give instructions for a total of four different coloured glazes.

1 Prepare the ground
Apply two base coats of eggshell paint allowing each to dry thoroughly (about 16 hours for each coat).

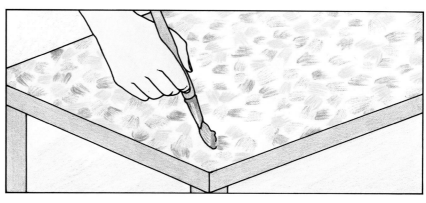

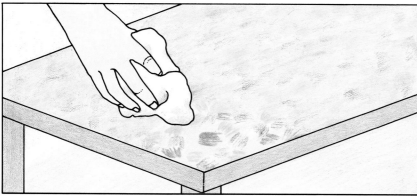

2 Apply the glaze △
Dip the larger artists' brush into the first batch of glaze and dot paint at random over the surface. Clean the brush with white spirit and repeat the process with second and third batches of glaze while the first is still wet.

3 Blend the colours ◁
Add a third colour if you want to. Then, using the lint-free cloth, gently blend the three colours together just enough to create a mottled background.

4 Spatter with white spirit ▷
Dip the smaller (soft) brush into the white spirit and hold it over the still-wet mottled surface. Tap it sharply on the straightedge so that the white spirit spatters the surface. Wait a short while between each spatter, as the white spirit does not take effect instantly, and you can only see how much the colour is being dispersed after a few seconds. Because the glaze is so slow drying, you can wipe over the surface and start again, if you are not satisfied.

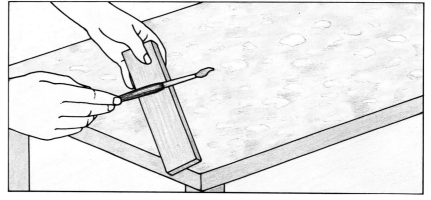

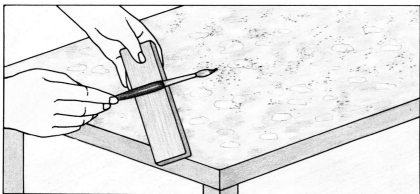

5 Spatter with colour ◁
Dip the same brush into the final batch of glaze and flick a fine spray of colour over the surface by tapping the stock of the brush on a straightedge, as before or use a stiff brush, and run your fingers over the bristles.

6 Paint in the 'veins' ▷
Wet the sword liner with white spirit and paint in the 'veins' of the stone. Outline the veins in a darker colour if you feel they are not clearly defined. Allow to dry thoroughly before coating with polyurethane varnish as for spattering.

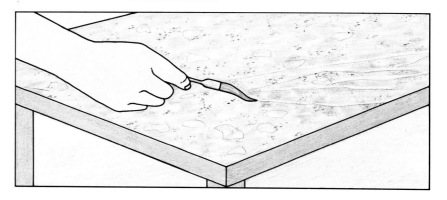

BRIGHT IDEA

Spattering fabric You can spatter fabric to match your decor. Choose a light-coloured natural fabric (such as sheeting or curtain lining) and use heat-setting fabric paint, watered down if necessary. Lay the fabric flat to spatter it. Experiment with different types of brushes: for example, try dipping a washing-up brush in paint and running your fingers through it. Press underneath a piece of scrap fabric to set the dyes.

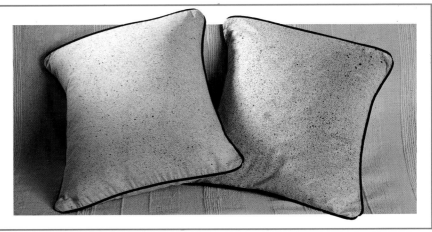

FLICKING

Flicking is a variation of spattering which combines streaks with spots. It is ideal for covering surfaces quickly. You can afford to load the brush more heavily and to be less precise.

1 *Prepare the surface* ◁
Start by painting the basecoat, then mask the areas which you don't want to paint. Thin the paint so that a streaky effect is created when it is flicked on the surface. Also use a slightly different technique: shake the brush with a flick of your wrist to achieve the desired freehand effect.

2 *Remove the protective paper* ▷
When paint is dry to the touch, remove the masking tape.

▽ *Stony look*
To imitate granite, this wooden box has been painted with a base coat of grey, and then cissed in pink and dark grey, and finally spattered with black.

MARBLED PAINT EFFECTS

Imitating the look of marble with paint is not difficult, as long as you limit yourself to small areas.

Marble has one of the most attractive natural finishes, and has long been admired by man. However, it does have disadvantages: it is heavy, expensive and cold to the touch. Perhaps it is for these reasons that painters have been imitating marble for thousands of years. When the work is done with real skill, it is almost impossible to distinguish a good fake from the real thing.

Such realism is beyond the capabilities of most amateurs, and many do not even attempt it. However, you do not need to be too ambitious. It is relatively easy to create the flowing, veined effect of marble without copying a particular piece of the stone.

Start by looking at as many examples of marble as possible, to give you a clear idea of the overall effect as well as the detailed colourings. It is often used for fascias on banks and offices, as well as fire surrounds and small pieces of furniture, such as washstands. Colours vary from creamy whites, rose, blue and golden marble to rich reds, greens and blacks. If you haven't got a suitable piece (such as a cheese stand or pastry slab) it is worth photographing any unusual marbles which interest you. Glossy magazines are another source of inspiration.

SURFACES TO MARBLE

The technique described here can be used for walls, woodwork, floors, or furniture, but before you embark on a large project, practise on small items – picture frames, boxes, or lengths of moulding for skirting boards or architrave, for example. This gives you a chance to try out different colours and effects, and mistakes on this scale are less disastrous than if you are working on a whole wall.

When working on larger items, remember that although you aren't going for a total trompe l'oeil effect, you should not defy nature. Only apply the technique to small areas – preferably surfaces which could conceivably have been constructed from stone. A table in a solid shape is a suitable choice: a chair with delicately-turned legs is not. Marble wooden skirtings and fireplace surrounds, but not doors or window frames.

Walls and floor can be marbled to great effect. Real marble usually comes in slabs, so it is a good idea to copy this effect on walls or floors. Divide walls into rectangular slabs and marble each one separately. Wood floors present the problem of how to cope with the boards: marble is never laid in planks. Even with the most careful filling the boards will probably still show. One answer is to cut plywood floor tiles and marble them individually, away from the site, before fitting them. Alternatively, lay large sheets of hardboard or squares of plywood on the floor before painting it. Varnish well to protect the work.

However adept you become at the technique, do use it with restraint. Marbling the whole of a small room in a strong colour can be oppressive: marbling just the dado, or fireplace and skirting, will be much more effective.

VEINING

The veins in marble run diagonally. They spread out rather like a series of rivers with lots of tributaries. These tributaries do not, however, simply peter out: they must rejoin the main 'river' or cross or join up with another system. If you are unsure of how much veining to put in, always err on the side of too little rather than too much. A restrained effect is far more attractive than an over-busy mess.

Marbled dado
Marbling the dado and skirting softens the whole look of a room. It is a practical finish too, as it helps to disguise lumps and bumps.

SURFACES AND MATERIALS

The preparation of surfaces and materials needed for marbling are much the same as for other paint effects.

Preparation Prepare wood surfaces as described on pages 17–18. Rub the surface over lightly with abrasive paper to give the surface a key.

Walls should be prepared as described in Preparing Walls, pages 7–10 for basic preparation tasks and Hanging Wallpaper, pages 61–64.

The base coat is two coats of oil-based eggshell paint. Brush strokes should not show, so rub down lightly with glass paper after each coat to ensure a smooth surface.

The glaze is the same as that used for creating other paint effects (see instructions on page 22). Artists' oil colours or universal stainers are used for tinting the glaze, with white oil-based (gloss or eggshell) paint added for pale or opaque colours.

Varnishing not only protects the surface, it softens the veining effect and gives the surface the satiny sheen that real marble has. Use satin finish varnish, applying two or three coats to woodwork and five to floors.

CHECK YOUR NEEDS
- ☐ Dust sheets/newspapers
- ☐ Masking tape
- ☐ Rags/paper towels
- ☐ Rubber gloves
- ☐ White spirit
- ☐ Paintbrush cleaner
- ☐ Glasspaper

For the base coat:
- ☐ Oil-based eggshell paint
- ☐ Selection of brushes for walls, woodwork, or furniture, as required.

For the top coat and veins:
- ☐ Transparent oil-based glaze
- ☐ White plastic paint kettle (or old ceramic dish)
- ☐ Artist's oil colours or universal stainers
- ☐ White oil-based paint for light or opaque colours
- ☐ Old saucer or bowl
- ☐ Old spoon
- ☐ Old artist's paint brush for mixing
- ☐ Scrap of paper for testing glaze
- ☐ Matt or silk varnish

For applying the paint:
- ☐ Paint brushes
- ☐ Pieces of sponge
- ☐ Pieces of lint-free rag
- ☐ Fine, soft artist's brush
- ☐ Newspaper
- ☐ Feathers or soft paint brush

WHITE MARBLE

This finish starts with a white or off-white base coat, which is left to dry. Successive subtly-tinted glazes are added, followed by veining. All these must be done in one session: do not work on an area which takes more than about half an hour to cover.

1 *Apply the base coat*
Apply a base coat of white or off-white eggshell finish paint (you can tint white paint with artist's oil colour to get the shade you want).

2 *Tint the glaze*
Mix up three gently-graded tones of transparent pale grey glaze, using artist's oil paints or universal stainers to tint the glaze. Thin the glaze with white spirit (about one part white spirit to two parts tinted glaze) to give a workable consistency.

3 *Apply the first coat* ▷
Paint a fine, even film of the palest glaze on to the surface. Use a bundle of rags to rag-roll the surface (see page 24).

This will lift off some of the grey glaze, leaving a very pale, two-tone surface. Leave to dry for about 1 hour, so that the surface is still very slightly tacky.

4 *The second coat* ◁
The second coat is 'ragged on' to the two-tone surface, to add further tones of grey. Dip a clean rag into the second batch of tinted glaze and wring it out. Bunch the rag into a loose bundle and press it lightly and quickly over the first coat. The preceding colours should still show through – you can leave quite large patches.

5 *Soften the effect* ▷
Immediately take a square of clean, dry rag about the size of a handkerchief, turn in the edges to form a smooth pad and pat it over the surface to soften the effect. Leave the surface to dry for about half an hour, so that it is slightly tacky.

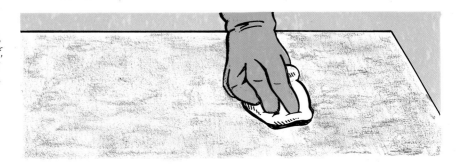

6 Apply the third coat
Apply a coat of the third and darkest batch of glaze in the same way as the second. Soften as before and leave to dry for about 20–30 minutes (so it is still slightly tacky).

BRIGHT IDEA

Papering over the cracks If you don't feel you can tackle marbling yourself, but like the effect, use a marble-effect wallpaper instead to cover boxes or table tops. Prime the surface, cover with paper using wallpaper paste, then apply two or more coats of satin-finish varnish to protect the surface.

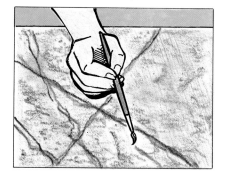

7 Add the veins ◁
Using artist's oil colours, mix up combinations of black, raw umber and white to give two tones of dark grey. Use a fine-pointed artist's brush to draw in the veins. Rotate the brush as you draw it across the surface to give you different thicknesses of line. (Professionals sometimes use the tip of a feather for very fine lines.) Paint in veins in both colours, bringing them close together at some points and creating a fine lattice in a single colour in other areas.

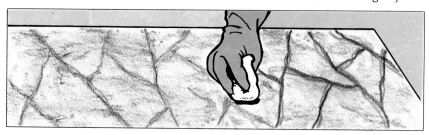

8 Soften the veins ◁
Make up a pad of clean cloth as before and pat it over the veins to soften them and blend them into the background. (Again, some professionals prefer to use the side of a feather to do this.) Allow the surface to dry completely.

9 Check the effect
If the veins are too soft, add an extra black or dark grey outline to some of them for a more defined effect.

10 Varnish the marbling ▷
When you are happy with the effect and it is dry, apply two or three coats of satin finish clear varnish. Allow to dry and rub down between coats.

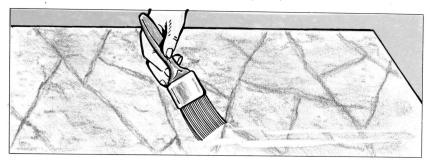

BLACK MARBLE
This is a very dramatic finish which should be used with discretion. It is effective when used in smallish amounts to contrast with paler marbles – on skirting and fireplace in a room with a rosy marble dado, for example, or as part of a pattern of marbled 'inlay'.

1 Apply the base coat
Prepare and prime the surface if necessary, then apply a coat of dark grey undercoat followed by one or two top coats of black oil-based eggshell finish paint.

2 Mix the glaze
This needs to be pale and opaque, so use a recipe of 1 part oil-based white eggshell to 3 parts glaze. Mix up with enough white spirit to give the consistency of single cream (roughly 1–2 parts white spirit to 4 parts tinted glaze).

3 Apply the glaze ▷
Use a sponge or a fairly large brush to apply the glaze randomly over the background, leaving some of the background colour showing through. You can leave quite large bands of black showing in some areas.

4 Breaking up the surface ◁
Scrunch up a sheet of newspaper and press it all over the surface to give a rag-rolled effect with a slightly veiny look. Change to a fresh sheet of newspaper when the first one becomes clogged with paint.

5 *Softening the effect ▷*
Take a square of clean, lint-free white cotton rag, turn in the corners to make a pad as before and pat it over the surface to soften it and merge the colours further. Allow to dry for about half an hour, so it is still slightly tacky.

6 *Add the black veins ◁*
Use a fairly fine, round artist's brush, or the end of a feather, to add a tracery of black veins, bordering and linking the darker background areas. Soften with a brush, cloth, or feather and allow to dry for about 15 minutes.

7 *White veins ▷*
Next add a tracery of white veins in the same way. They should run quite close to the black veins, and merge into them slightly. Marble of this type often has fairly large white areas, so paint in some diamond-shaped patches along the veins. A touch of green, added to the paint used for the veins, can look particularly effective.

8 *Varnish the marbling*
When you are completely happy with the effect, apply two or more coats of clear, satin finish varnish, rubbing down between each coat.

▷ *Slate grey and smart*
This redundant fireplace has been given a simple wooden surround. The surround and a wooden 'hearth' have been treated along the lines described here to give a slate-grey marbled look.

IMITATING TORTOISESHELL

The rich, almost translucent, tones of tortoiseshell can be achieved using traditional paint techniques.

Tortoiseshelling, like marbling, does not have to be a slavish copy of the real thing. It is, however, a good idea to look at examples of real tortoiseshell before you start work. The range of colouring occurring in the natural material is quite extensive – from two-tone blackish-brown and beige, to tawny gold and blond shades as well as quite red ones.

SURFACES TO PAINT
Flat or slightly curved surfaces are on the whole best for tortoiseshelling. This enables you to get a satisfying 'flow' to the pattern. You will also have a more realistic effect as real tortoiseshell could not have been used for exaggerated curves or intricately carved surfaces.

Real tortoiseshell was used in relatively small amounts, for inlay, on small panels, boxes, or the backs of hair brushes and mirrors. The fake finish, therefore, is usually used in the same way.

This is a lovely way to decorate a plain box, perhaps 'inlaying' the top in a blond tortoiseshell and using an auburn tortiseshell for the border and on the sides. Picture and mirror frames, too, look sumptuous tortoiseshelled. Small, plain lamp tables can be treated in this way, or you could 'inlay' the top of a larger table. Tortoiseshell the frame or, better still, the panels of a door; not both. Take it off its hinges first as it is easier to work flat.

Tortoiseshell can also be combined with other finishes such as a plainish marble or simulated ivory.

You can, however, put realism aside and go for an over-the-top treatment. Choose a piece of junk furniture for this – an old dining table or wood-framed chair. This can make a stunning focal point in a room. Don't make the mistake of tortoiseshelling more than one such piece. A tortoiseshell dining table and simple black chairs can look stylishly unusual; a complete dining set plus sideboard will give you indigestion!

Creating the effect The tortoiseshell pattern should run diagonally across the work with bands of colour diverging slightly. You should therefore always work in a diagonal direction when building up the pattern.

Isn't it rich?
Tones of dark oak, with the addition of earthy-coloured oil paints are the main ingredients of this paint effect, imitating the look of tortoiseshell. Several coats of varnish create a deep, protective sheen, enhancing the effect.

PAINTS AND VARNISHES

As long as you have gathered together all the materials you need, the actual task is not too difficult.

Paints Oil-based eggshell is used for the base coat and artists' oil colours for the tortoiseshell pattern. The colours used depend on the final colouring you want to achieve; the base coat is usually quite a strong chrome or acid yellow, with streaks of oil paint in dark tones; black, burnt umber, indian red, and so on.

Varnish This finish relies heavily on a very glossy appearance for its impact. There is no such thing as matt tortoiseshell. Coloured varnish is the medium in which the effect is created and additional layers of clear gloss varnish give the essential glowing transparency. The varnish can be thinned with white spirit to help the colours 'flow'.

Varnish dries quite quickly so it is essential to work fast. For this reason, don't work on too large an area at once. If you intend to cover a large area, divide it off into panels. Work on alternate panels, leaving each to dry before tackling the ones between.

PREPARATION

Prepare the surface carefully, filling any cracks and rubbing down thoroughly to get as smooth a surface as possible. Prime and then give the surface one or two coats of oil-based eggshell in the chosen colour.

By varying the colour of your base coat and using different shades of varnish and artists' oil colours you can create a spectrum of different tortoiseshells. Try out the effect on a sample board before starting work in earnest.

CHECK YOUR NEEDS

For the base coat
- ☐ Oil-based eggshell paint (yellow)
- ☐ Paint brush of appropriate size

For the finish
- ☐ Medium oak and clear gloss varnish
- ☐ White spirit
- ☐ Artists' oil colour
- ☐ Paint kettle for the varnish
- ☐ Saucers for the oil colour
- ☐ 2 × 5–10cm paint brushes
- ☐ 2 × 12mm artist's soft brushes
- ☐ Clean rags
- ☐ Plastic sheets/newspapers

CISSING

Horizontal surfaces can be cissed to 'open up' the colour and give an interesting, antique effect.

Load an artist's brush with white spirit and tap it against a stick held over the wet surface of the work. It takes a few seconds for the effect to become noticeable so beware of becoming over-enthusiastic. Tap lightly, leave for half a minute, then repeat if necessary. (For further details, see Speckled Paint Effects pages 29–32.)

DARK GOLD TORTOISESHELL

The whole of the table in the picture was given the same dark gold tortoiseshell finish. When completely dry, and before varnishing with clear gloss varnish, the framework around the edge of the top of the table was given two coats of thinned dark oak varnish to 'hold' the centre. The side panels and legs were darkened in the same way. Chrome yellow, oil-based eggshell paint was used for the base coat. You will also need medium oak varnish, black and burnt umber artist's oil paints.

1 *Apply the base coat*
Prepare the surface, prime and give it two coats of yellow oil-based eggshell. Leave to dry.

2 *Apply a coat of varnish* ▷
Thin the medium oak varnish with white spirit in the ratio of three parts varnish to one white spirit. Apply liberally to the surface.

3 *Break up the surface* ◁
Straight away, tease the brush over the varnish to cover the surface with irregular diagonal zig-zag bands. This gives an uneven background, imitating the irregular patches of natural tortoiseshell. Do not allow to dry.

4 Dab on darker colours ▷
Thin each of the artists' colours with a little white spirit. Then, still working in a diagonal direction, add squiggles of burnt umber to the wet surface. Then add blobs of black. You can also add touches of unthinned dark oak varnish.

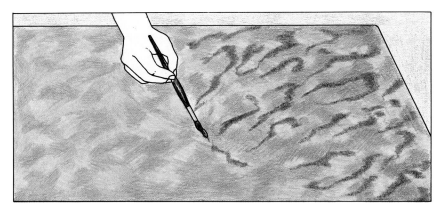

5 Soften the effect ◁
Soften and blend the blobs of colour into the varnish by stroking a clean, dry brush gently over the surface. Work in the same diagonal direction as before. Soften further by flicking the brush vertically, working even more lightly and gently. Then repeat the process diagonally once more.

6 Ciss the surface ▷
If you want to break up the pattern you can ciss the surface while it is still wet. Load a small, round artist's brush with white spirit and ciss very sparingly over the surface.

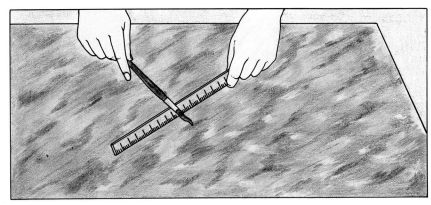

7 Soften the cissing ◁
Use the dry brush again to soften out any hard lines created by the cissing, working in a diagonal direction as before. You should now have a surface resembling tortoiseshell. If you are not happy with it, add further touches of oil colour and soften as before.

8 Apply protective varnish ▷
When the work is completely dry, finish with several coats of clear gloss varnish. The more coats, the more luxurious and light-reflecting is the final result.

VARYING THE EFFECT

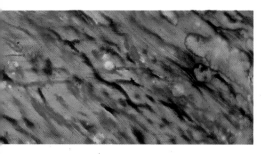

△ *Tortoiseshell with a touch of red*

△ *Blue/green tortoiseshell technique*

△ *Crimson/oak tortoiseshell effect*

The method of creating dark gold tortoiseshell can be adapted to give a whole range of natural-coloured tortoiseshells. All you need to do is to change the colours used for the base coat, varnish and squiggles.

Sample boards It is a good idea to try out different effects first – particularly when experimenting with fantasy colours – before starting work in earnest. Make a series of sample boards like the ones shown on the left and note down the colours that you use, for further reference.

A pale tortoiseshell is achieved with light oak varnish and raw umber and yellow ochre artist's colour over a pale yellow base coat. Dark oak varnish over bright sunshine yellow or brick red with raw umber and black artists' colour will give richer, darker tortoiseshells. The sample at the top, on the left, is painted on a canary yellow base. A wash of medium oak varnish was used, with 'blobs and squiggles' of light red and

burnt umber. The very bright yellow, coming through the rich oil colours, creates a warm, glowing effect.

Fantasy effects In addition, you can adapt the tortoiseshelling technique to give a whole range of fantasy effects.

Try tortoiseshelling over colours other than yellow – a bright mid blue or emerald green. On these colours use medium or light oak varnish and black and a chestnut red mixed from vermilion and light red artists' oil colours. For an even more unusual effect, use one of the new coloured varnishes, which are available in around 40 colours.

The two samples on the left are created as follows;

Blue/green sample. Pale, grey-blue base coat, lime green polyurethane varnish, with Cerulean blue, Viridian green and Paynes grey oil colours.

Crimson/oak sample: Warm, flesh-pink base coat, medium oak varnish, with Alazarin crimson, Rose pink and Flake white oil colours.

△ *Don't forget what the real thing looks like.*

BRIGHT IDEA

TORTOISESHELL FRAMES
Turn a wide, plain wooden picture frame into something unique and special by giving it the tortoiseshell treatment. This gives you an ideal opportunity to experiment and practise the technique. The darker colourings work particularly well on frames. You could make up a whole series of frames in different effects, including fantasy ones, instead of sample boards.

Similarly, experiment with other small items, such as wooden hairbrushes or small trays.

▷ *Traditional appeal*
A very traditional look demands attention to detail; colour-washed walls, wood-grained doors and tortoiseshell-effect architraves and cornices, together with massed objets d'art create an extravagant confusion in this living room.

40

PAINT EFFECTS ON WOOD

Furniture and woodwork can be given a rich and original look by dragging or combing in attractive colours.

Most of the broken paint finishes that are applied to walls can be used with equal, if not greater, success on woodwork and furniture. Two paint techniques that are particularly suited to wood are dragging and combing. Both add an interesting depth and texture and are well worth the effort involved.

DRAGGING

This subtle, wood grain effect with finely graduated lines is made by drawing a long-bristled brush through wet glaze to reveal some of the paler base coat colour underneath.

This is one of the most difficult paint effects to do well on a large surface as it requires a very steady hand. So, although it can produce some elegant results on walls, it's a good idea to master the technique first on smaller surfaces such as furniture and mirrors or picture frames.

Dragging also looks good on woodwork, especially when combined with other paint treatments on walls (such as sponging or ragging) but is too subtle to be effective on floors.

Proper dragging brushes, made of long and flexible bristles, are the easiest to use and give a very professional finish, but they are very expensive.

For woodwork and furniture, you can substitute a small oval varnish brush or ordinary paint brush and get perfectly good results. A 100 or 125mm paint brush, a wide paper-hanging brush or a painter's dusting brush, can also be used to drag walls.

COMBING

This is similar to dragging but bolder and coarser, and easier for a beginner to handle. In this case a hard comb-like object is raked through wet paint to make regular stripes or diagonals, or a pattern such as fan shapes or waves. The size and scale of the pattern is dictated by the size and spacing of the teeth and to a certain extent by the material of the comb.

The strong lines created by the comb make this an excellent technique for large painted areas such as floors. Perhaps because it lacks subtlety, combing is rarely used on furniture and woodwork, although it can be very effective if used with conviction.

The choice of tools for combing is wide. Ready-made steel and rubber combs are available in various shapes and sizes and are relatively cheap to buy. If they are hard to track down there are alternatives. An Afro hair comb does the job well, or you can make your own comb from a suitably rigid material.

COLOUR SCHEMES

To show up clearly, the dragged or combed colour must be darker than the base colour: either a deeper tone of the base colour, or a colour over white or cream. It's generally best to pick a stonger colour than you think you need for the top coat as the final result is usually quite a bit paler.

Combed texture
Special steel combs are sometimes used to emphasise the grain of course-textured woods. Here, the tongued-and-grooved panelling and skirting board are combed in deep blue over a paler blue which just shows through.

PREPARATION AND PAINTS

Prepare wood surfaces, priming bare wood where necessary. Then lightly rub down the surface with glasspaper to give a key before applying the base coat.

If you are going to drag the walls, prepare them in the usual way, hanging lining paper if the plasterwork is uneven or cracked.

The base coat for dragging or combing should be one or two coats of oil-based eggshell paint. Eggshell doesn't normally need undercoat, but bare wood must be primed.

The top coat for dragging is the traditional transparent oil glaze that is tinted to the right colour and diluted with white spirit until it is a workable consistency.

Glaze is also suitable for a combed surface. Or you can use an oil-based eggshell paint: either straight from the tin, or thinned with up to 25 per cent white spirit but make sure that the paint is thick enough to cover the base coat properly.

Varnish After the paint finish has dried, it is advisable to protect it with several coats of clear matt or semi-gloss polyurethane varnish.

Dragged woodwork ▷
Dragging is an elegant finish that is particularly suited to formal rooms. Here, a delicate green glaze brushed over a pale background emphasises the horizontal lines of the skirting.

CHECK YOUR NEEDS
☐ Dust sheets/newspaper
☐ Masking tape
☐ Rags/paper towel
☐ Rubber gloves
☐ White spirit
☐ Paint brush cleaner/restorer
For the base coat:
☐ Primer and/or undercoat
☐ Oil-based eggshell paint
☐ 50-75mm paint brush for woodwork/furniture; 100mm brush for floors/walls
☐ 19mm cutting-in brush (for woodwork/furniture)

For the top coat:
☐ Transparent oil glaze plus: white plastic paint kettle; universal stainer/artists' oil colour for tinting glaze; white oil-based paint (for light colours); saucer or bowl; old spoon; narrow long-handled paint brush for mixing; scrap paper for testing glaze OR
☐ Oil-based eggshell paint

For the finish:
☐ Dragging brush (or 50-75mm varnish brush or ordinary paint brush for woodwork; paperhanging brush or 100-125mm paint brush for walls)
☐ Matt or semi-gloss polyurethane varnish for protecting the finish, and varnish brush OR
☐ 50-100mm paint brush for applying the top coat
☐ Bought or home-made comb

▽ *Dragging brushes*

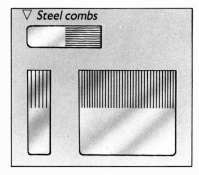

▽ *Steel combs*

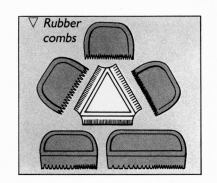

▽ *Rubber combs*

DRAGGING WOODWORK

Taking off fine stripes of wet glaze to reveal a paler base coat gives a subtle textured finish which works well on woodwork and complements walls that are decorated with other paint finishes.

Brushwork The most important point to watch with dragging on wood is to follow the direction of the wood grain. So, skirting boards, for example, and other horizontal pieces of woodwork are painted and dragged horizontally.

With doors, follow the normal sequence of painting (see page 20). If the door is panelled as on the right, brush vertically on vertical mouldings and inset panels, the central and outer vertical sections, and on both sides of the door frame; brush horizontally on horizontal mouldings and sections, and along top of frame. Work on one section at a time, and mask adjacent sections with masking tape.

1 Apply the glaze
Use a fairly narrow brush to apply a fine, even film of glaze in the direction of the wood grain. Don't try to cover too large an area in one go or the glaze dries before you can drag it.

2 Drag the glaze
Take a fairly narrow brush, and draw it through the wet glaze in the direction of the wood grain. After each stroke, wipe the brush clean on a rag or waste paper.

Keep your strokes as straight and steady as possible. You'll find this easier to do if you hold the brush lightly and just skim the bristles over the wet surface – if you grip the brush tightly and press too hard, you can get wavy lines.

3 Repeat the technique
Stop dragging the first section of glaze just short of the wet edge. Then brush glaze on to the next section so that it overlaps just a little with the first, and continue dragging the wet glaze for a regular striped effect.

If you're painting a panelled door, allow each section to dry completely before repeating steps 1 and 2 on an adjacent section.

4 Varnish
Leave the dragged glaze until it is thoroughly dry. This usually takes at least two days. Then apply one or two coats of clear matt or semi-gloss polyurethane varnish to protect the decorative finish.

This is especially important on such things as wooden doors and cupboards, as they get a great deal of daily wear and tear.

BRIGHT IDEA

MARK UP A PANELLED DOOR

For added visual interest, you can emphasize the structure of a panelled door by marking the joins or joints between horizontal and vertical sections after dragging, but before varnishing them.

Using a metal ruler and fairly blunt knife, lightly score a line along the joins between horizontal and vertical sections on the door. Then use a sharp lead pencil to fill in the scored lines, or apply a fine line of oil-based paint in a slightly darker tone than the dragged colour. Emphasize the mouldings by making the internal angles darker in the same way.

DRAGGING ON WALLS

The method for dragging walls is basically the same as for woodwork but, as the surface is very much larger, it really needs two people to do the job – one person to apply the glaze, the other to drag it before it dries. You also need to use wider brushes.

To help keep your dragged lines straight, use a plumb line and chalk to make vertical guidelines at intervals across the wall.

1 Apply the glaze
Starting in one corner of the room, use a wide paint brush to apply a thin, even film of glaze in a 50-60cm wide strip from top to bottom of the wall.

2 Drag the glaze
Draw the dragging brush (or a suitable substitute) through the glaze from top to bottom of the wall, easing the pressure on the brush at the end of a stroke to prevent a build-up of glaze. Wipe off smudges with a rag dampened with white spirit.

If the wall is too high to drag in one easy movement, drag down from the ceiling to about waist level: then drag up from the skirting, and feather the join. Stagger the joins to avoid a noticeable ripple across the wall.

COMBING

This is a bold finish that gives scope for some very dramatic effects, and it's a good idea to spend time experimenting with different combs. For example, you can create all sorts of effects by combing in first one direction, then crossing these lines with others. If you intend to do a lot of combing, it's worthwhile making a sample book and noting how different patterns are achieved.

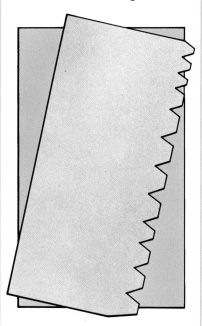

BRIGHT IDEA

Make you own comb by cutting V-shaped slots into a piece of hardboard, plastic or rubber flooring – or any similar semi-rigid material. A comb cut from a rubber window-cleaning

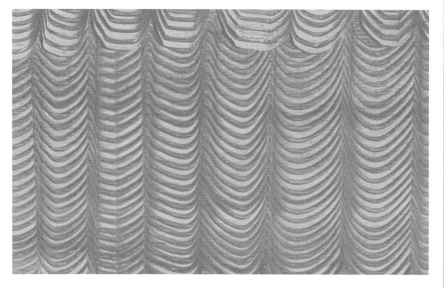

1 *Apply the paint or glaze*
Work in sections that can easily be combed while wet, and apply a fairly thick but even layer of paint or glaze, following the wood grain. If you're painting floorboards, start in the corner farthest from the door and work on a couple of boards at a time.

2 *Comb the paint or glaze ▷*
Draw the comb firmly through the wet paint or glaze to create a pattern of straight lines, waves, semi-circles or what you will.
Wipe the comb clean with a rag every so often. If you're covering a largish area, wrap a rag round the comb to soak up some of the displaced paint.

3 *Varnish*
Once the combing coat is dry, protect the finish with at least two coats

of clear polyurethane varnish. Three coats of varnish provides better protection for floors.

squeegee, for example, is particularly easy to use on floors because of its ready-made handle.

Cut several combs with teeth of various widths to alter the scale

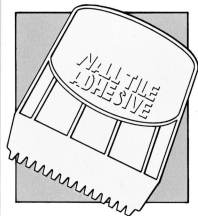

of the pattern, making sure that teeth are spaced widely enough for the combing to show up. Try, too, cutting notched teeth of different widths on one comb for an interesting effect.

If you don't want to go to the trouble of making a comb, you could adapt a hair comb, or improvise with a simple item such as a tile adhesive spreader, available from any good DIY shop.

PAINTING STRAIGHT LINES

Once you've got the knack of using a brush correctly painting is child's play…until you come to the edges.

The only remotely difficult thing about painting is achieving a neat straight edge. For example, painting window frames and glazing bars is difficult enough to do neatly in itself. But the paint should extend on to the glass (both inside and out) by about 3mm to seal the junction between putty and glass so that condensation or rainwater cannot run down between the two and rot the frames. Getting a straight edge on the face of the glass is even harder to do freehand, especially if you are a beginner. The end result is often wobbly edges that simply look amateurish.

Similar problems arise when you're painting walls and ceilings a different colour, painting skirting boards, or if you want each side of a door to match the colour scheme of the room it faces. Here you do at least have a sharp angle between the surfaces – an internal one between walls and ceilings or skirting boards, an external one on door edges – but it can still be difficult to leave a straight paint line along it.

The last decorating area where you might want to paint neat straight lines is if you are being creative – for example by decorating walls or furniture with bands of contrasting colour. Here even a steady hand may not be good enough to give good results. You need some help.

TOOLS AND MATERIALS

There are several tools that make painting straight lines easier, and one invaluable material.

Cutting-in brush Basically a slim paint brush, this has bristles cut across at an angle instead of dead straight. It's mainly used for painting internal angles and you use it by drawing the edge of the brush with the longer bristles along the angle. However, this still takes a steady hand, so it is of limited use to the beginner.

Paint shield This is a metal or plastic plate which you hold so that its edge marks the line up to which you want to paint; at the same time it masks the surface you want to protect. It takes some practice to get good results as it is all too easy to get paint on the edge or underside of the shield and smear it where you don't want it.

The paint shield is most useful for jobs like painting skirting boards, as it holds the carpet away from the board while you work.

Paint pad Designed for painting along

Band aid
Bands of white on plain Wedgwood blue walls form dramatic frames for the window, picture and vanitory unit.

the angle between wall and ceiling or wall and skirting board, this has small guide wheels along one edge. You run these against the surface you're not painting, while the pad applies the paint to the one you are. The result is an edge that will be straight so long as the surface the wheels run against is true. If it isn't – which is often the case – the paint line will follow its contours and end up looking a little wavy.

Masking tape The most versatile aid of all for the sort of jobs described earlier is masking tape, a paper tape with a low-tack adhesive on the back used to mask any surfaces you don't want to paint. Stick it into position with one edge along the boundary line where one colour finishes, then paint up to that line, allowing the paint to overlap on to

the tape. Peel the tape off carefully to leave a perfectly straight edge.

If you are painting with strong colours and want to butt a second colour neatly up to the edge of the first, stick tape along the edge of the area you've just painted (when the paint's dry) and repeat the process.

To use masking tape successfully, first make sure that it's well pressed down on to the surface it's masking, or paint will tend to creep under the edge. Running over the tape with a seam roller before you start painting takes care of this. Second, don't leave the tape on too long, nor try to remove it too soon. Wait until the paint is touch-dry, and then peel it off by drawing the tape away from the painted area in a continuous motion. Third, if

you need to mask over a freshly-painted surface, wait until the paint is hard-dry (overnight for gloss, four hours for emulsion) before you apply the tape. Otherwise paint and tape may peel away together.

You can buy masking tape in a variety of widths; 25mm is generally the most useful. But if you are using a spray gun to paint sections of colour, or painting a wall with a paint roller, which emits a fine spray of paint, use one of the wider tapes to protect the surrounding areas.

Dispenser Also on the market is a hand-held dispenser which applies a strip of brown paper to the surface you're masking, sticking it in place automatically with ordinary masking tape as you run the dispenser along the surface (see **Bright idea**, page 48).

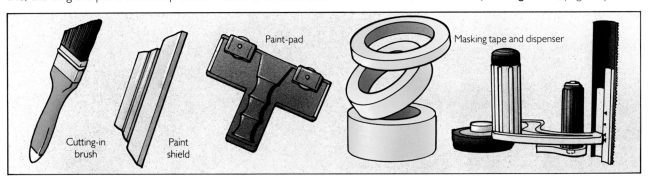

Cutting-in brush   Paint shield   Paint-pad   Masking tape and dispenser

(see **Bright idea**, page 48).

CHECK YOUR NEEDS
- ☐ Painting equipment
- ☐ Cutting-in brush (optional)
- ☐ Masking tape, seam roller and sharp craft knife
- ☐ Paint shield OR
- ☐ Special paint pad with roller guides

MASKING WINDOWS
When applying the final coat to window frames make sure that the paint spreads a few millimetres on to the glass. This ensures that the putty is completely sealed and waterproofed. Stick masking tape on the glass, set slightly away from the timber, to make it an easy job and obtain a perfect finish.

1 Prepare the surface
Start by washing down the paintwork thoroughly, using a fungicide or diluted household bleach (1:4 with water) to kill mould spores. Sand with fine wet-and-dry abrasive paper, used wet, to provide a key for the new paint. Rinse and leave to dry. Finally clean the window panes.

---

2 Stick the first piece of tape ▷
Cut a strip of masking tape a fraction longer than the width of the pane and stick it to the glass parallel with the top edge, about 2 or 3mm from the angle. Press it down firmly by hand, and use your craft knife to cut the ends of the length so they finish 2 or 3mm in from the sides of the pane. Then peel back one end of the tape by 40mm.

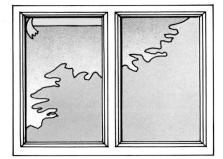

3 Add the next piece
Apply the second length of tape to one of the side edges of the pane, overlapping it on to the stuck-down end of the first length. Press it down and trim as before.

Apply the third length along the bottom edge of the pane so that one end overlaps the end of the second length. Trim the end neatly as before.

4 Finish taping ◁
Finally stick the fourth length in place and trim it as before. Then stick the peeled-back end of the first length over the stuck-down end of the final one. The reason for applying the tape in this sequence is that it makes it much easier to strip the tape off after you've finished painting – see Step 6.

Repeat the procedure for all the remaining panes.

5 Paint the window frame
Check that all the tape edges are firmly stuck to the glass. Then start painting, using either a narrow ordinary brush or a cutting-in brush. Tackle each masked edge first, then paint the rest of the glazing bar or frame next to it before moving on to the next section. Don't apply the paint too thickly, and brush it out well (unless using gel paint) or you'll get unsightly runs.

6 Remove the tape ▷

When you've finished, leave the paint until it's touch-dry (at least four hours for gloss, two for eggshell). Then use the tip of your craft knife to lift the last end of the tape to be stuck down. Lift it carefully so you don't mar the still-soft paint. Once you have raised it enough, peel the tape away by pulling the end towards the centre of the pane.

As you reach the corners, the overlaps you so carefully formed earlier will lift the next lengths cleanly away. Just change the angle of pull so you're always drawing the tape at an angle towards the centre of the pane.

PAINTING DOORS

If you're painting the two sides of a door in different colours you'll be faced with two long edges where the colour changes. This means you'll have to take particular care when painting them.

1 Decide which colours to use ▷

The convention is that you paint the opening edge of the door (nearest the handle) the same colour as the face that opens into the room, and the hinged edge to match the other face. This ensures that when the door is open the visible edge and face match in each room.

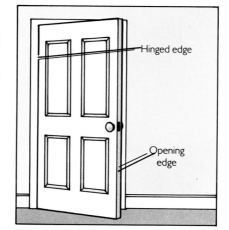

2 Prepare the door

Start by wedging the door open. Always unscrew all the door furniture – it's time-consuming and fiddly to paint round it and you usually end up with paint on the handles however careful you are. Then clean down the existing paintwork as for windows – wash down, sand lightly, rinse and allow to dry.

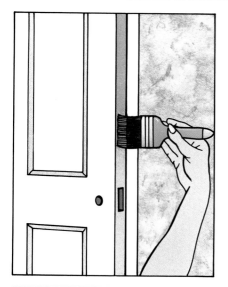

3 Paint the edge of the door ◁

There's no need to mask an external angle such as the edge of the door before you start painting; the sharp angle acts as a guide so long as you apply the paint correctly. Always draw the brush across the surface towards the edge where the paint changes colour, using very little pressure as the bristles reach it. Then allow the bristles to run off the edge, and lay off the paint in the usual way with a final light brush stroke parallel with the edge. If you draw a loaded brush across the corner, you will 'scrape' a thick layer of paint off the bristles, and the result will be unsightly runs and a build-up of paint.

4 Paint the face of the door

Paint one edge of the door first, then its matching face. Wait until the first colour is touch-dry before changing colours and painting the other face and edge (if this is necessary). Keep children and pets away until the paint is dry.

Then replace the door furniture, using new screws if the old ones are mangled. Leave the door wedged ajar at least overnight, otherwise the still-soft paint is likely to stick to the frame, ruining the finish.

PAINTING SKIRTING BOARDS

If the walls are painted, rather than papered, it is a good idea to mask the wall when painting the skirtings. Also, if you have polished wood or vinyl floors or carpets which cannot be lifted, these should be protected.

1 Mask the wall

Mask the join between skirting boards and walls by applying tape to the wall surface before you start painting.

Of course, if you're painting them before hanging wallcoverings, masking won't be necessary; simply take the paint on to the wall surface by about 12mm so that any uneven trimming of the wallcovering won't leave bare plaster visible.

2 Mask the floor

Use masking tape along the angle between skirting board and floor if you have a 'hard' floorcovering – vinyl, cork, woodblock and the like. If you have carpet, it's better to use a paint shield to hold the fibres away from the board as you paint it. Move it along as you complete each section. Strips of thin cardboard tucked under the skirting board will do just as well, and you can leave them in position until you've finished to stop the fibres getting stuck to the wet paint. Alternatively, you can buy special carpet shields which you slip in and leave until the paint is dry.

PAINTING PATTERNS

Masking tape is the perfect ally for painting bands of colour or creating geometric patterns on walls or furniture. Don't forget that the tape may lift freshly-applied paint if you use it to apply second colours before the first are really hard. This means waiting overnight for gloss paint and at least four hours with emulsions. Use chalk, a straightedge and a draughtsman's square to transfer the patterns you want to the walls.

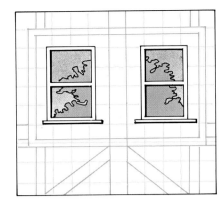

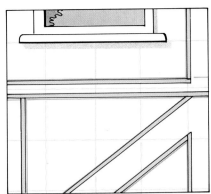

1 *Plan the pattern*
Plan out your design on paper first, unless it's very simple. It's best to use graph paper so you can scale the plan up to cover the actual surface you're decorating. For a simple band of colour or a straightforward shape you can of course apply masking tape and work out the design directly on the wall.

2 *Transfer pattern to the wall △*
With a graph-paper design, decide how many times you need to enlarge it and draw a grid on the wall. If the final pattern is to be ten times larger than the original drawn up on graph paper with 1cm squares, then each one will be 10cm square. Transfer the design to the wall one square at a time.

3 *Apply the first strips of tape △*
Next work out the order in which you will apply the bands and areas of colour. Remember that you need to wait for one area to become thoroughly dry before applying masking tape over it and painting the adjoining area. Apply the first lot of masking tape, lining up its edge with the design, and start painting.

4 *Peel off the tape ▷*
When you've completed painting all the areas in the first colour wait for the paint to become touch-dry and strip off the tape pulling it gently away from the freshly painted area. Unless you're working with emulsion paint it's best to wait overnight before applying more tape over the fresh paint and carrying on with the design.

5 *Repeat the process*
Carry on applying tape, painting, leaving the paint to dry and then peeling it off until you have completed the patterns. Remove any chalk marks.

▽ Stunning stripes
Short broad stripes wrapped round the edge of a chimney breast wall form a simple but most effective design.

BRIGHT IDEA

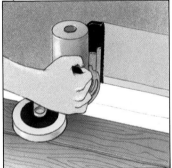

Spray painting Ordinary masking tape is fine for most painting jobs, but if you're using a spray gun for speed and quality of finish you really need a wider band of paper to stop the paint mist getting where it shouldn't. You can do this by sticking strips of newspaper or polythene in position with masking tape, but it's fiddly. The answer is a dispenser called a Paper Taper, which automatically applies a strip of brown paper (150 or 300mm wide) to the surface you want to mask and sticks it in place with masking tape as you move along the wall or door.

USING READY-MADE STENCILS

Stencilling is a simple and exciting way of adding colour and pattern to furniture, walls, and even floors.

A stencil is essentially a decorative cut-out through which paint is brushed on to the surface beneath. It can be used to add just as much or as little pattern as you like – a simple one-colour border, for example, or a more intricate overall design in several colours. The real charm of stencilling is its simple hand-done look so don't worry if you make the odd mistake.

Ready-made stencils are mostly available in simple folk style with lots of birds and floral motifs. You can also make your own stencils to complement existing furnishings.

Buying stencils Most stencils are made from stencil card or acetate sheet. Card is strong and good for large designs; acetate is more expensive but it is transparent which makes it much easier to position stencils accurately.

Some ready-made stencils are pre-cut, ready to use; uncut (ready-to-cut) stencils are cheaper but less convenient. They are available from specialist suppliers (often mail-order) and some art and craft shops.

The background Almost any surface will do as long as it's clean, sound and smooth: avoid irregular surfaces as paint tends to creep under the stencil.

If you're painting walls for stencilling, use emulsion paint. Use a mid-sheen oil-based paint, such as eggshell, on wood; full gloss provides less key for the new paint.

Colour schemes Try out alternatives on scrap paper first. Then paint a test stencil and fix it with masking tape to the surface you're stencilling to see if the effect really works.

PAINT AND BRUSHES

Paint The best paints for stencilling are water-based – they're fast drying so there is less risk of smudging and you can work faster.

Water-based acrylic colours are ideal and come in a wide colour range – most art shops stock tubes of acrylics. Ordinary emulsion paint is almost as good. A 'test' pot should be sufficient for a small stencilling job or use any left-over paints that you have.

Oil-based eggshell paint is most suitable for stencilling on woodwork but takes longer to dry.

A stencilling brush, with stiff bristles cut squarely at the end, gives an attractive finish that is softly stippled. A good alternative is a blunt-ended hoghair artist's brush.

Both are available from most art and craft shops. Buy a brush for each stencil colour: small brushes for small designs, bigger ones for large designs.

Clear polyurethane varnish is essential protection for stencils on wooden objects, furniture and floors. You'll need at least two coats of varnish on furniture and up to five coats on floors. A satin finish is suitable for most purposes.

stencil brush

A co-ordinated look
A single motif in one colour is used to decorate walls and soft furnishings.

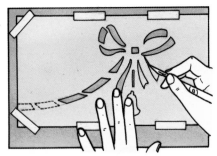

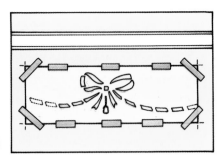

Cutting out stencils △

Uncut stencils are supplied with areas marked for you to cut.

Fix the stencil securely to a cutting board with masking tape, then use a sharp knife or scalpel to cut out the areas to be painted. Cut out any small detailed sections first.

Take your time. To avoid jagged edges, always draw the knife towards yourself and keep going for the entire length of a cutting line. When cutting curves, turn the board rather than the knife for a smoother cut.

If the stencil is made of card, finish off by smoothing down any rough edges with very fine glasspaper.

1 Prepare to paint △

If stencils are well spaced out, a saucerful of paint will probably be enough for the whole job.

Put a small amount of acrylic colour or paint into the saucer. Whatever paint you use, it should be creamy, not watery – watery paint tends to seep under the stencil and smudge. If necessary, thin acrylic colour with a little water and mix well with an old teaspoon; thin oil-based paint with a little white spirit.

2 Fix the first stencil △

Decide where you want the stencil and lightly pencil in the position; for marking out a border (see page 52).

Then smooth the stencil on to the surface, and fix in place with small strips of masking tape. When fixing on to paint or paper, remove some of the tape's stickiness by pressing it on to your forearm a few times.

Register marks If you're using stencil card and stencilling more than one colour, lightly pencil round the top corners of the first stencil. You can then match the corners of subsequent stencils to these marks.

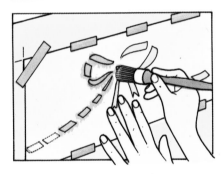

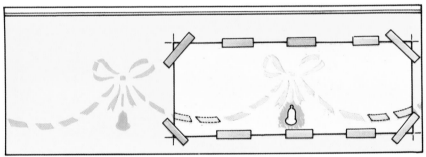

3 Paint the first colour △

If you're using two or more colours, the rule is to stencil all of one colour before going on to the next.

Dip just the end of the brush into the first colour, and remove excess paint on scrap paper. Then dab paint on to the cut-outs, working from the edges to the middle of each. To stop paint seeping under the edges, gently press the stencil flat against the surface with your free hand – or with a wide-bladed knife if it's easier.

4 Remove the stencil

Leave the paint to dry for about a minute. Then carefully remove masking tape and lift the stencil off. Don't slide it or the wet paint will smudge.

5 Finish the first colour

Complete the design in the first colour. At regular intervals, wipe the stencil and the brush clean with tissue or a rag moistened with water (or white spirit for oil-based paint) to prevent a build-up of paint.

6 Paint the second colour △

Let the first colour dry completely, then start again with the next colour.

Carefully position the second stencil. With acetate, align the printed register marks on the stencil with the painted design on the wall. With card, match top corners of stencil with the pencil marks on the wall.

Tape stencil to the surface and, using a clean brush, apply paint as for the first stencil. Repeat this step if using more than two colours.

CHECK YOUR NEEDS
☐ Craft knife and spare blades
☐ Scalpel for intricate work
☐ Cutting board – eg offcut of chipboard or plywood
☐ Masking tape

For painting the stencil:
☐ Paint
☐ Stencil brush for each colour
☐ Old saucer and teaspoon
☐ Scrap paper
☐ Pencil and rubber
☐ Masking tape
☐ White spirit (if you're using oil-based paint)
☐ Plenty of rags or paper towel

For marking out wall borders:
☐ Plumb line and bob (or any small weight and fine cord)
☐ Set square or T-square
☐ Ruler or straightedge
☐ Spirit level
☐ White chalk and pencil

Cleaning up
As soon as stencilling is completed, clean brushes and stencils. For cleaning off water-based paint, all you need is plenty of water. Remove oil-based paint with white spirit; wash brushes out in soapy water and rinse.

Gently wipe stencils clean with a rag or paper towel dipped in water or white spirit, taking care not to catch any fragile cut-outs that might tear. Store stencils flat when dry, separated with sheets of tissue or greaseproof paper.

Finishing off
When stencil paint is dry, use a rubber to remove any pencil marks.

If you are protecting stencils with polyurethane varnish, allow two to four days for the paint to dry completely before applying several coats of varnish.

USING A STENCIL BRUSH
Don't overload the brush with paint: use it almost 'dry'. You can always make a stencil print darker, but it's difficult to lighten it once paint is applied.

Dip just the end of the brush into the paint, then stamp on to scrap paper to remove any excess paint. Holding the brush at right angles to the surface being painted, work from the edges of the cut-out to the middle with a firm dabbing motion to reduce the risk of paint seeping under the edges of the stencil. Gradually build up soft translucent colour leaving the middle of the cut-outs a bit lighter than the edges to create shading.

STENCIL BORDERS

A stencil can be used to add decoration in exactly the same way as a wallpaper border.

For measuring and marking out a horizontal border design, follow the steps below. Be prepared, however, to make adjustments visually – few walls are absolutely even, and corners are rarely right angled.

1 *Mark a vertical line* ▷
Use a plumb line and pencil to mark a vertical line on the wall – just below the ceiling, or just above picture rail or skirting level, depending on the position you want the border.

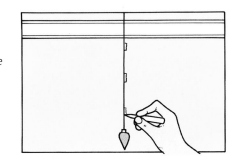

2 *Mark a horizontal line* ▷
Using the ceiling angle, picture rail or skirting as a base, measure along the vertical line and mark with chalk or pencil the point where the top edge of the stencil will come. (If the border is to be at ceiling level, the top of the stencil should be a few millimetres below the ceiling to allow for any deviation. If it's at skirting or picture rail level, the bottom

of the stencil should be a few millimetres above the board or rail for the same reason.)

Position a set square or T-square at this point and mark off a horizontal guideline at right angles to the vertical line. Use a metal ruler to continue the line along the wall and right round the room.

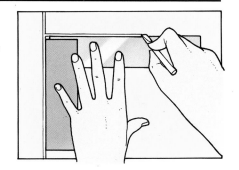

MARKING THE POSITION OF STENCILS

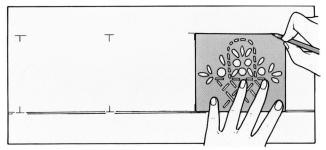

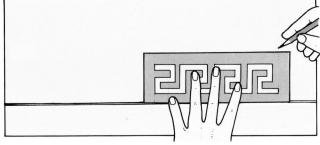

A regular motif pattern △
A regular motif looks best if it's spaced out evenly. Measure the length of each wall and divide by the length of the stencil to give you the number of complete motifs that will fit along each wall.

Plan on squared paper how the stencil design fits the wall space, taking into account any spacing between motifs. Then mark the position of motifs along the horizontal guideline by pencilling in the corners of each stencil – work out from the centre of a wall in both directions to distribute the motifs evenly.

A continuous pattern △
With a continuous pattern, such as the greek key shown, lightly mark the first and last cut-outs in the stencil on to the wall with pencil. Working clockwise round the room, move the stencil along to overlap the last outline on the wall with the first cut-out in the stencil. Draw in the last stencil cut-out and continue round the room.

If you're using two or more colours, you will also need to pencil in the corners of the first stencil as a register for subsequent stencils.

Turning a corner △
With a continuous pattern, you may need to take the stencil round corners. Score the stencil lightly along a straight edge with the back of a scalpel blade, then bend it over the straight edge to make a smooth fold.

Paint corner stencils last, but pencil in position of each one before continuing along the next wall.

BRIGHT IDEA

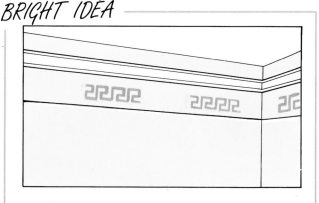

PAINTING A BORDER STENCIL

As you work along a border, make sure that you never place the stencil on top of wet paint. To avoid smudging the paint, do every second stencil and fill in the gaps later when the paint has completely dried.

MAKING YOUR OWN STENCILS

Making a stencil to your own design is an ideal way to add an individual decorative touch to a room.

Although there are dozens of ready-made stencils that you can buy, making your own gives you the opportunity to create a unique design that fits in perfectly with the style of a room. This chapter gives a step-by-step guide to making a stencil. For painting stencils, see Using Ready-Made Stencils.

Design ideas You can draw your own designs freehand, or you can copy motifs from almost anywhere. Books, for example, provide illustrations of flowers, animals and children's storybook characters. Lettering is another attractive possibility, or you might 'borrow' a design you like from a wallpaper, fabric or embroidery.

Don't be too ambitious to begin with. It's the shape, rather than the detail, that creates the decorative impact, so choose a well-defined motif that can easily be adapted for stencilling in one or two colours. You can then get away with using one stencil plate which is easier than using different stencils for different colours (see page 56).

Design and colour sense Some designs may need to be enlarged for use, while very large designs need to be reduced. You can do this by dividing your traced design into a grid, then re-drawing it to a suitable scale on squared graph paper (see overleaf). It may be easier, if you have access to a machine, to get a photocopy made to the size you want.

A balance of colour is important in stencilling so try out alternative colour schemes on scrap paper first. Then, to make sure the size of the design and your colours work, paint a test stencil on to paper and fix with masking tape to the surface you're stencilling.

TOOLS AND EQUIPMENT

You will need stencil brushes and paints, preferably water-based. For making the stencil itself, you will also need the following.

Stencil material Traditional stencil card is like cardboard but has an oiled surface that doesn't soak up paint; it's strong, so good for intricate designs or very large stencils.

Acetate sheet is a little more expensive but has the advantage of transparency which allows you to trace designs directly on to it as well as line up separate stencils for multi-coloured designs. It is also slightly easier to cut, but needs handling with care as it is liable to split on sharp corners and curves.

Card and acetate are available from most art and craft shops.

A fine-tipped felt pen to mark the design on stencil card; on acetate, use a permanent marker that will not smudge on plastic.

A cutting board – a piece of smooth chipboard or plywood makes a good flat surface for cutting on. If you're going to do a lot of stencilling, you can buy special cutting boards from art shops.

A sharp knife to cut the stencil – a craft knife is suitable, though a scalpel gives better control on fiddly work. You will also need plenty of spare blades – a blunt knife can easily tear the stencil as you cut.

Dressing up
This white-painted dresser has been transformed with a stencilled pattern of summer garlands and fruit.

CHECK YOUR NEEDS

For copying the design
☐ Tracing paper
☐ Pencil
☐ Graph paper for enlarging/
   reducing

For making the stencil
☐ Stencil card
☐ Carbon paper
☐ Fine knitting needle
☐ Fine-tipped felt pen
OR
☐ Acetate sheet
☐ Fine-tipped permanent marker

For cutting the stencil
☐ Offcut of chipboard or
   plywood or a cutting board
☐ Craft knife and sharp blades
☐ Scalpel for intricate work
☐ Nail punch or knitting needle
   for punching out circles
☐ Fine-grade glasspaper to
   smooth edges of stencil card

For painting the stencil
☐ Paint
☐ Stencil brush for each colour
   or small sponge
☐ Fine artist's brush for
   touching in
☐ Old saucer and teaspoon
☐ Scrap paper
☐ Pencil and rubber
☐ Masking tape
☐ White spirit (if you're using oil-
   based paint)
☐ Plenty of rags or paper towels
☐ Polyurethane varnish and
   varnish brush (optional)

BRIGHT IDEA

Sponge it If you don't want to
invest in a special stencil brush,
cut up small pieces of sponge or
foam and use them to dab on
colour instead.

Use one end of the sponge for
one colour, then let it dry and use
the other end for a second
colour. Make sure that you don't
overload it with paint.

ENLARGING AND REDUCING

If motifs taken from books or prints
need to be enlarged or reduced, either
use the method detailed below or have
a photocopy made to the size required.

Trace the motif
First, trace the motif on to tracing
paper as shown in Step 1, opposite.

Then, using a ruler, draw a frame
closely round the traced motif and mark
this area off into regular squares; an
easy way of doing this is to stick the
framed tracing on to graph paper (with
glue or double-sided tape) so that you
can use the squares as a guide. Lastly,
carefully cut round the frame of the
squared motif.

TO ENLARGE

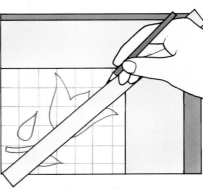

1 *Draw a diagonal △*
Place the squared motif in the
bottom left-hand corner of a large
sheet of tracing paper – this must be at
least as big as the finished stencil.

Draw a diagonal line from the
bottom left-hand corner of the traced
motif through the top right-hand
corner, extending it across the sheet of
tracing paper underneath.

Remove the tracing of the motif.

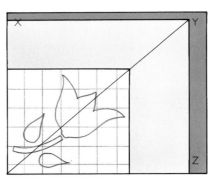

2 *Draw a larger frame △*
Decide how large you want the
stencil to be and mark the desired
height on the left-hand edge of the large
sheet of tracing paper, X.

Draw a horizontal line from X to cut
the diagonal line at Y. From Y, draw a
vertical line down to the bottom edge
at Z. You now have a scaled-up frame.

3 *Copy the design △*
Divide the new scaled-up frame
into the same number of squares as the
original small one. The squares will, of
course, be proportionately larger.

Then carefully copy the motif, square
by square, on to the scaled-up grid. It
helps to first mark where the main lines
of the motif intersect grid lines, then join
up the marks.

TO REDUCE

1 *Draw a diagonal △*
Stick the tracing of the motif over a
piece of graph paper, draw a frame
closely round the motif and cut out.

Place a small sheet of tracing paper –
at least the size of the finished stencil –
in the lower left-hand corner of the
framed motif. Draw a diagonal line from
the bottom left-hand corner to the top
right-hand corner of the framed motif.

2 *Draw a smaller frame*
Decide on the new height of the
design and mark the top right-hand
corner of the smaller frame on the
clean tracing paper at X. Join this point
to the side and bottom edges of the
small frame, Y and Z.

3 *Copy the design*
Divide this area into the same
number of squares as the original motif.
Then copy the motif square by square
on to the scaled-down grid.

MAKING A STENCIL

If you are using acetate, and your chosen design does not need enlarging or reducing, you can trace the design directly on to the stencil material.

1 Trace the design

Place your chosen design on a flat surface and lay the tracing paper (or acetate) on top. If you're tracing from fabric, stretch the fabric out on card and fix with pins or tape first.

Then use a soft pencil (or permanent marker on acetate) to outline the parts of the design suitable for cut-outs, making sure that the sections separating one cut-out from another (the 'bridges') are wide enough to hold the stencil together.

2 Colour code the tracing

If the design incorporates more than one colour, colour-code the tracing with pencils or crayons and keep it for reference when painting.

In any case, keep the tracing so that you can cut a fresh stencil if the first one gets damaged.

3 Transfer the tracing

Position the tracing on the card or acetate to allow for a wide margin round the stencil design – see Step 6.

If motifs are to be repeated so close together that part of one is covered up as you stencil the next (eg, a border), include the covered part of the design on the card or acetate and use as a guide for lining up the stencils.

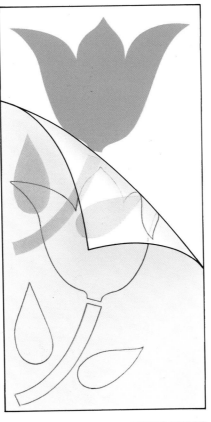

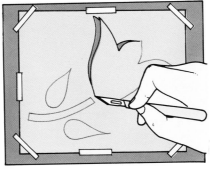

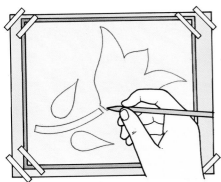

Stencil card △ Place tracing (right side up) over stencil card, with a sheet of carbon paper sandwiched in between, and fix layers in place with tape.

Go over the outlines of the design with the tip of a fine knitting needle. Then remove tracing paper and carbon, and mark the design on the stencil card clearly with a fine felt-tip pen.

Acetate Fix the traced design (right side up) to a flat surface with masking tape. Lay a sheet of acetate directly over it, secure with tape, and draw the outline with a permanent marker pen.

4 Cut out stencil △

Practise cutting on a spare piece of card/acetate before starting on the stencil itself.

Then place the drawn up stencil on the cutting board, and fix it in place with masking tape if you find this easier. Use a sharp knife or scalpel to cut out areas to be painted; use a nail punch or knitting needle to punch out small dots and circles.

Cut out small detailed sections first and larger areas last to avoid weakening the stencil.

Always draw the knife towards yourself, applying even pressure for the entire length of a line so that you get a clean edge. When cutting curves, turn the stencil material slowly round rather than the knife.

5 Tidy up the edges

When you've finished cutting, use the knife to carefully trim any jagged edges. Smooth down rough edges on stencil card with fine glasspaper.

If you accidentally tear the stencil, repair it with clear, self-adhesive tape on both sides. Then trim away excess tape with a sharp knife, making sure that it doesn't overlap on to the edges of the cut-out.

6 Cut stencil to size

Finally cut the card/acetate to size leaving a frame of at least 25mm all the way round the design, otherwise the stencil will be weak and floppy.

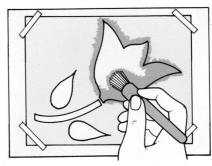

7 Paint the stencil △

Tape the stencil to the wall with small strips of masking tape. (If you press the tape on to your forearm to get rid of some of the stickiness, it will be less likely to damage the wall decoration when you remove it.) Dip just the end of the stencil brush into the paint, removing any excess on scrap paper so that the brush is almost dry. Then dab paint on to the cutouts, working from the edges to the middle of each.

If you're using several colours, do all of one colour before going on to the next. You can use masking tape to keep areas clean and separate: paint in one colour, allow to dry, then change the masking tape without removing the stencil from the surface being painted.

8 Fill in detail

When you've filled in all the cut-out areas, leave the paint to dry for a minute, then carefully remove the tape and lift the stencil off. Don't slide it or the paint may smudge.

Use a small artist's brush to fill in any missed edges and give the finishing touches to the design.

9 Clean up

As soon as stencilling is completed, clean brushes out in the appropriate solvent: water for water-based paints, white spirit for oil-based paints.

Wipe stencils with a rag dipped in solvent and store flat when dry, separated with tissue or greaseproof paper.

MULTI-COLOURED STENCILS

If a fairly complicated design is to be stencilled in several colours, it may be easier to cut a separate stencil for each colour. In this case, you will need registration marks on the stencils so that you can line them up on top of each other during painting.

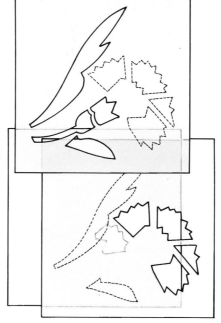
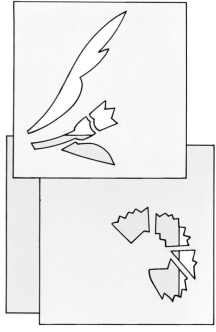

Colour wise △
The carnation motif is stencilled in spring green and two shades of pink.

Borrowed style ▽
Inspiration can come from anywhere. Here, the carnation-ribbon theme was taken from the upholstery fabric, as were the soft colours. The large stencilled bow makes a pretty feature.

Acetate *As you trace the separate colour areas on to different sheets of acetate, draw in a few dotted lines of other parts of the design so that you can check the exact position of each stencil in turn when you come to painting.*

Stencil card *Trim tracing and sheets of card to the same size before transfering the different parts of the design. Leave a margin round the design for strength.*

Then match up the corners of tracing and card as you transfer the separate colour areas to the different stencils. When you come to painting, pencil round the top corners of the first stencil so that you can align subsequent stencils.

PAINTING MURALS

Add fun to a featureless room by painting the walls – with cartoon characters or a touch of realism.

Long before man had mastered making paper or canvas they drew on the nearest available surface – the wall. So murals were the first wall decoration and the first paintings. From these early drawings, artists developed and refined their techniques, so that in renaissance times some of the world's greatest works of art were murals. However, when it comes to painting your own murals, a sense of humour or of style is more important than technical skill.

TYPES OF ROOM
Like any other dominant decoration, murals are best confined to rooms where they will retain their novelty value. The playroom or a child's bedroom, the bathroom and dining room are all obvious choices, and murals can also be used to transform gloomy halls and stairways and basement kitchens.

Consider any room without interesting features, particularly if it has a dull outlook, but only paint a mural in rooms which are in constant use if you are confident it won't pall.

COLLECTING IDEAS
Before preparing the walls, you must decide on the finished effect and subject matter you want to paint. Decide whether you want a series of pictures to cover the whole wall, a joky detail, an architectural effect (such as a mock cornice or false fireplace) or wall to wall decoration. A term you may come across used to describe wall paintings is

trompe l'oeil – a French phrase used to describe a picture which deceives the eye. Most trompe l'oeil effects do require a certain amount of skill, and involve more advanced paint techniques, such as marbling and wood graining.

A straightforward pictorial design is the easiest to achieve. The simplest have a picture book quality – one reason why murals are so suitable for children's rooms! Choose a theme which has large areas of flat colour, like a Noah's ark, farm landscape, or seaside scene. Two-dimensional cartoon characters also translate easily on to walls – and you have the advantage of plenty of reference material to give you ideas. Look at illustrations in comics or books when you are planning the design.

For a more sophisticated effect, look at your own holiday snaps: a view over tiled roof-tops, a haphazard mediterranean village, or an exotic beach scene can all be effective. Cloud formations can be imitated on ceilings to create a restful effect in a bedroom or bathroom (where you are likely to spend some time looking at the ceiling).

If you want to create an amusing effect, there are some simple trompe l'oeil ideas you could try. Paint or stencil a vase of flowers above a shelf, or a pair of candlesticks and a clock above a mantelpiece. Brighten up a blank wall by painting a window with a view, or add pot plants, creepers and palms growing up from the skirting, with birds and butterflies for extra realism.

Architectural details are a form of trompe l'oeil which require a certain amount of skill. For inspiration, look at the wallpaper friezes available from smarter interior decorating shops, and at pictures of rooms with cornices, dado rails and so on. The two-dimensional representations will help to show you how to handle the lighter and darker colours to create a three-dimensional effect. You should also master some of the more advanced decorating techniques, such as marbling, before attempting to paint imitation fireplaces on your walls.

A repeat pattern, stencilled or painted freehand, though not strictly a mural gives wall-to-wall decoration with a rich, tapestry effect far removed from the regular, mass-produced and often slightly hard look of wallpaper.

Add a smile
Children's rooms are an ideal place to practise your skills. Start with simple shapes, like the pie and 24 blackbirds, and if you are pleased with the result, go on to paint other nursery rhymes.

PREPARING THE SURFACE

Prepare the wall to suit the style of the design. Whatever the base surface you choose, the wall should be sound and fairly smooth, with no peeling paint or crumbling plaster. Most effects look best applied directly to the wall, rather than to lining paper. However, if the surface of the wall is poor, carefully hung lining paper, sealed with a thin coat of wallpaper paste before painting the base coat, gives a sound base.

A classical mural looks effective on a subtly shaded background which adds depth and richness. Traditionally, paints were not available in large quantities, accurately tinted by the manufacturer, so imitate the gentle effects of hand-mixed paint with one of the following techniques: apply a base coat of pale emulsion, with a slightly darker coat on top, sanded down finely to give the effect of a fresco (an Italian wall painting applied to wet plaster). For a translucent look, apply a coat of eggshell topped by a pale tinted oil-based glaze.

Stippled or sponged base coats also create background interest to the subject of your mural.

Landscape murals look particularly effective painted over a colour-washed wall (see pages 25-28). Use colour shading for sea or sky scenes.

Nursery murals in bright primary colours with clean outlines should be painted on smooth walls, with a base coat of silk or matt emulsion paint.

Surrounding walls which are not to be covered with the mural need to complement it, so it's a good idea to paint them to match the base on which the mural is painted.

Painting woodwork Mural techniques can be adapted to decorate furniture or doors. If you want to try out your skills first to see the effect, start by decorating a table or chest. The item should be primed, undercoated (two coats) and a base coat of oil-based gloss or eggshell paint applied before you start work. You will have to use oil-based paints on top of the base coat.

PAINTS AND MATERIALS

The paints you use depend on the final effect you are after. Usually when painting murals you don't need large quantities of paint, but you do need a fairly large range of colours. In most cases it is best to use emulsion paint: you have to wait for one colour to dry before applying the next, and emulsion is quicker-drying than oil-based paints. (However, if the base coat is gloss or eggshell, you will have to use oil-based paints.) The problem is that emulsion comes in a limited range of rather soft colours, so you may need to mix your own colours.

You can tint emulsion paint yourself, using stainers, or economize by using small sample pots. Quick-drying artist's acrylic colours will give you a wider choice of colours, but these can be expensive used over a large area, and may be difficult to obliterate if you eventually want to paint over the design.

Equipment You will need graph paper to draw up the design, and chalk, a plumb line and pencils to transfer it to the wall. As well as the usual brushes for painting the base coat, you will need a wide selection of brushes for painting the design, including a tapered cutting-in brush for large areas, and artists' brushes and a lining fitch (a smaller version of a cutting-in brush) for details. Finally, you will need a new, fluff-free paintbrush for the protective coat of varnish.

CHECK YOUR NEEDS
- ☐ Paper and pencil
- ☐ Steel rule
- ☐ Paint for base coat
- ☐ Brush or roller
- ☐ Chalk
- ☐ String, plumb line and bob
- ☐ Selection of wall and artist's brushes
- ☐ Emulsion and artist's acrylic paints or oil-based paints
- ☐ Damp sponge
- ☐ Varnish and brush

Optional:
- ☐ Fine artist's brush and black paint
- ☐ Natural sponge
- ☐ Stencilling equipment

DRAWING UP THE MURAL

Collect together your ideas for the mural (pictures from books, photographs, postcards) before deciding exactly how it should look. Then measure up the wall and sketch out a plan before drawing up the mural.

1 *Choose your subject matter*
You probably have a fairly clear idea of what you want to paint, but it is advisable to collect lots of pictures together to give you examples of the details: a book of illustrated nursery rhymes for a child's bedroom, glossy magazines with traditional interiors for trompe l'oeil fireplaces, and so on.

2 *Paint the base coat*
When you have collected the ideas together, you can decide on a background colour. It's a good idea to collect plenty of paint charts so as to check that you'll be able to get hold of the coloured paints you need. Prepare the wall, filling cracks and sanding it smooth, and apply the base coat.

3 *Measure the wall*
Measure up the wall to be painted, and draw a plan of it. Sketch in the effect roughly on your plan: if you are copying directly from a picture or series of pictures, make sure they will fit the space you have, and decide where each picture should be positioned on the wall.

4 *Draw up a grid ◁*
Draw a grid over the picture you are copying or draw up the design on graph paper. The scale of the grid will depend on the amount you need to blow up the picture. If you are blowing up a postcard-sized picture (10cm by 15cm) to go on a wall 240cm by 360cm, a 1cm square grid is a good size.

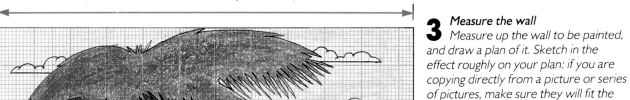

5 *Mark the grid on the wall ▷*
Draw up a grid on the wall scaling up the squares to fit the space. In the example here, you should draw the lines 24cm apart. Use the plumb line and bob to get the lines straight, marking the wall with chalk, which can be wiped off easily. An easy way to mark the wall is to cover a length of string with chalk, pin it to the wall at each end of the line you want to mark, then snap it so the chalk marks the wall.

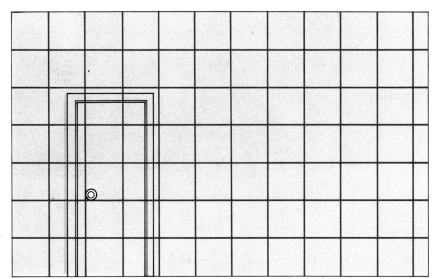

6 *Transfer your picture to the wall*
Look at each square of your original picture carefully, and copy it on to the corresponding space on the wall. Again, use chalk, which can be wiped off easily. Step back from the picture to check the overall effect, and smooth out any jerky lines. It is a good idea to complete your sketch a couple of days before you paint, so that you can come back to it and check the effect.

PAINTING SIMPLE SHAPES

Cartoon characters or a simplified landscape in areas of flat colour are fairly straightforward to paint, once you have transferred the picture on to the wall.

1 *Choose the first colour ▷*
Decide which colour to paint first: it is a good idea to start with the larger areas. Starting at the top of the wall, paint all the areas which are to be that colour. Allow to dry. It may help to put a tiny spot of colour in each area before you start so that you don't miss one. If you need to mix different shades of the same colour, start with the darkest shade, and gradually add more white.

2 *Add the next colours*
Continue in this way until the mural is complete, applying two coats to cover the grid marks where necessary, and allowing each colour to dry before painting adjacent areas.

3 *Clean the wall*
When the paint is dry, wipe away what remains of the grid with a sponge.
When you are happy with the effect, varnish the wall to protect the painting. Use clear varnish with a dash of white eggshell paint – this helps to prevent the varnish yellowing.

FINISHING TOUCHES

1 *Bold outlines △*
Use black paint to outline the characters, and give them greater definition. Outlining also helps to neaten any irregularities where areas of different coloured paint meet.

2 *Adding eyelights △*
A dot or crescent of white paint in the middle of an eye will give extra life to the eye. Position the light patch so that it looks as though it is a reflection from the window in the room. (You can even paint 'window pane' highlights in the eyes.)

3 *A three-dimensional look △*
Make apples look round and characters look fat by creating shadows and highlights: mix darker and lighter tones of the colour to be shaded, and sponge on the colour to give a gently graded effect.

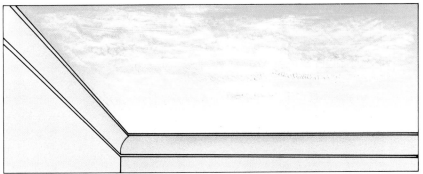

4 *Trompe l'oeil sky △*
Create a soft, summer sky by sponging clouds on to a pale blue background. Touches of pale salmon pink added to the edge of the clouds will imitate an evening sky.

BRIGHT IDEA

Even outlines A simple way to get bold outlines of images is to use a felt-tip pen: use a black, spirit-based marker which will not smudge. Test the effect of varnish over the lines before marking the wall, to ensure it will not run.

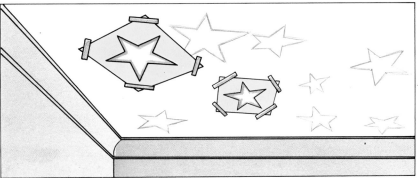

5 *Repeating images △*
If images are repeated on your design – simple flowers and leaves, birds or stars, for example – you can cut a stencil to make it easier to draw them. When using stencils in this way, don't just create the regular, border effect normally associated with stencilling: use the stencil as a template, drawing in the outline of each shape with chalk, and turning it to avoid regimented rows of shapes.

▽ Undersea world
Create a wet-look bathroom by painting the ceiling to look as though it is the surface of the sea. Add coral and a diving helmet – or just stick to simple goldfish.

HANGING WALLPAPER

If you are turning your decorating skills to wallpapering, be patient and methodical and you will get first class results.

Wallpaper can transform a room with colour and pattern and texture. It can also be the best solution for disguising less than perfect walls. So, if this is your first attempt at wallpapering, here's how to do it step by step.

Preparation The surface to be decorated should be clean and as smooth as possible. Old wallcoverings are best removed and damaged plasterwork repaired. For the basic preparation tasks, see Preparing Walls.

Seal new plaster with a thin coat of size – this will give the surface some 'slip', making it easier to slide the paper into place, and will ensure a good bond. Sizing can be done several days or about an hour before hanging the wallpaper.

Apply size (a watered-down adhesive) with an old paintbrush, and wipe off any drips as you go with a damp cloth (it is difficult to remove when dry).

Lining paper Plain lining paper can be used to improve uneven or cracked plasterwork and provide a good clean surface for new wallpaper. It comes in various grades: as a guide, use a light grade under ordinary wallpaper and a heavier one for rough surfaces and textured wallcoverings. There is also a grade called Finished Extra White especially for painting over.

Choosing wallpaper Avoid cheap thin papers – they can stretch and tear easily when hanging. The best choice is a medium-weight paper, either plain, textured, or with a small random design (it is much more tricky to match up a large pattern). Textured 'relief' papers are useful for covering up bumpy walls.

This chapter covers all the steps for hanging ordinary wallpaper that requires pasting. There are also ready-pasted papers. These are more expensive but less messy to use: lengths of paper are cut as for ordinary wallpaper but they only need to be soaked in water for a few minutes before hanging.

TOOLS AND EQUIPMENT

For hanging ordinary wallpaper you will need the following:

A table for marking up and pasting lengths of wallpaper. A fold-up pasting table is useful and quite cheap, but any table about 2m long can be used.

Size – a paste-like product for preparing bare walls. Although it can be bought, most wallpaper pastes can be diluted to make size following manufacturer's instructions.

Wallpaper paste usually comes as a powder for mixing with water. Any paste will do for ordinary paper; for vinyls and other washable papers use a paste containing a fungicide.

Plastic bucket for mixing paste (a wooden spoon or stick for blending).

A pasting brush for applying paste to the paper – an old 100mm paintbrush is ideal.

A paperhanging brush with soft bristles to smooth the paper on to the wall. For washable papers, a dry sponge can be used instead.

A measuring tape for measuring wall height and lengths of paper – a retractable steel one is useful.

A plumb bob and line for hanging wallpaper vertically. Any small weight attached to cord will do.

Scissors – use long-bladed scissors for cutting lengths; short-bladed ones (or a craft knife) for trimming.

A seam roller to smooth the edges of lengths firmly to the wall. Do not use on embossed papers.

A sponge or plenty of rags for cleaning up any splodges of paste.

A stepladder long enough to reach the top of the wall comfortably. Two stepladders and a plank are ideal.

For ready-pasted paper you will need a plastic trough for soaking rolled-up lengths of paper (usually supplied with the paper). A tube of latex glue is useful for finishing off any edges that come unstuck.

Share the load

The job of wallpapering is very much easier if there are two of you to share the workload. One person works at the pasting table, while the other hangs the wallcovering.

CHECK YOUR NEEDS

- ☐ Wallpaper
- ☐ Lining paper (if necessary)
- ☐ Paste
- ☐ Size (if necessary)
- ☐ Steel tape measure – and pencil
- ☐ Plumb line (or weight and cord)
- ☐ Table for laying out and pasting
- ☐ Long-bladed scissors for cutting lengths
- ☐ Small scissors or craft knife for trimming
- ☐ Plastic bucket
- ☐ Pasting brush (or 100mm paintbrush)
- ☐ Paper-hanging brush (or sponge for washable papers)
- ☐ Sponge and old rags for cleaning
- ☐ Seam roller
- ☐ Two stepladders and plank

HOW MANY ROLLS DO YOU NEED?

Estimate rolls needed by measuring the height of the room from skirting to cornice or ceiling and the distance round the walls.
This chart is calculated for standard wallpaper which is sold in rolls approximately 10·05m long and 530mm wide.

WALLS height from skirting	DISTANCE AROUND THE ROOM doors and windows included																	
	9m	10m	12m	13m	14m	15m	16m	17m	18m	19m	21m	22m	23m	24m	26m	27m	28m	30m
2·15-2·30m	4	5	5	6	6	7	7	8	8	9	9	10	10	11	12	12	13	13
2·30-2·45m	5	5	6	6	7	7	8	8	9	9	10	10	11	11	12	13	13	14
2·45-2·60m	5	5	6	7	7	8	9	9	10	10	11	12	12	13	14	14	15	15
2·60-2·75m	5	5	6	7	7	8	9	9	10	10	11	12	12	13	14	14	15	15
2·75-2·90m	6	6	7	7	8	9	9	10	10	11	12	12	13	14	14	15	15	16
2·90-3·05m	6	6	7	8	8	9	10	10	11	12	12	13	14	14	15	16	16	17
3·05-3·20m	6	7	8	8	9	10	10	11	12	13	13	14	15	16	16	17	18	19

Buy all wallpaper at the same time, checking that batch numbers are the same to avoid colour variations.
If the paper has a large pattern repeat, buy an extra roll.

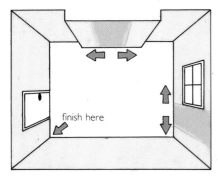

1 Plan your starting point △

Start alongside the largest window and plan to work away from the light, so that if any edges do overlap they will not cast a shadow and won't be so obvious.

Large-patterned papers, however, should be centred on a main focal point such as a fireplace and subsequent lengths hung working outwards in both directions.

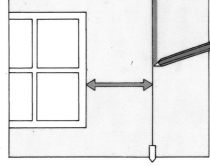

2 Mark a vertical guide line △

From the window frame measure out a distance of 15mm less than the width of your paper. Then use a plumb line and pencil to mark a vertical line down the length of the wall against which to hang the first length of paper.

This will ensure that it is hung absolutely straight and allow for any deviation in the window frame edge.

3 Measure for length

Measure the vertical guide line, and add an extra 100mm to the measurement to allow for trimming the paper at top and bottom. (Use this measurement to cut all the full lengths of paper.)

Lay a length of wallpaper face up on the table and measure out the first length. If it has a distinctive pattern, always ensure that a full pattern repeat is at the top of the wall where it will be most obvious.

4 Cut paper to size

Mark a cutting line in pencil across the paper (check it is at right angles to the edges) and cut along it with long-bladed scissors.

5 Match the pattern

Before cutting subsequent lengths with a straight match pattern, match them with the first length. Pencil 'top' on the back to avoid hanging patterns upside down. Keep leftovers for short lengths – over doors, etc.

If the paper has a drop pattern (on a diagonal), instead of a straight match, work from two rolls. If you cut alternate lengths from each roll – 1,3,5 from the first; 2,4,6 from the second, etc – the pattern should match more economically. Number as they are cut to keep them in order.

6 Paste the paper ▷

Lay the first length face down on the table – with the top end of the paper aligned with the end of the table and the long edge fractionally overlapping the side of the table farthest from you. Start pasting from the centre, working outwards and away from you to spread the paste evenly right up to the far edges.

Then move the paper towards you so that the paper overlaps the front edge of the table and brush towards you to get a good covering of paste on all edges.

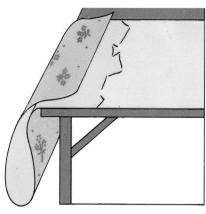

7 *Fold the pasted section* △
When the area of paper on the table has been pasted, fold this neatly in half with pasted sides together. Move the folded section along the table so it hangs over the edge and paste the rest of the paper in the same way.

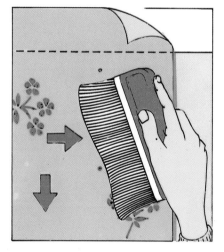

10 *Brush on to the wall* △
Use the paper-hanging brush (or sponge for washable papers) to press the paper against the wall – brush down the centre, then firmly out towards the edges. If the paper bubbles or wrinkles, gently peel it away to release the air and brush back into place. Unfold the lower half and brush out in the same way.

12 *Hang the second length* ▷
Hang the second length in the same way, butting the edges together. Match the pattern if there is one by sliding the paper up or down using the palms of your hands. Brush into place and trim as before.

8 *Lift the paper* △
When pasting is complete, fold the second half over, leaving a gap of about 50mm in the middle.
Some papers must be left for a few minutes for the paste to soak in or they will wrinkle when hung – follow the instructions on the roll label. Lay this paper to one side and paste the next length in the meantime.
When the paper is ready to be hung, drape it over your arm, as shown, to carry it to the wall.

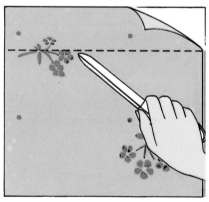

11 *Trim the edges* △
Press the top edge into the angle of wall and ceiling or cornice with the back of a scissors' blade. Peel back the paper, cut along the crease, and use the tip of the hanging brush to dab the end of the paper neatly back into place.

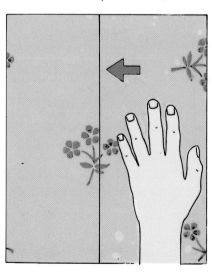

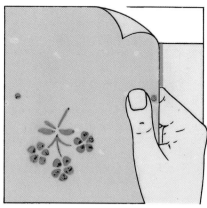

9 *Hang the paper* △
Use a stepladder to reach the top of the wall. Unfold the upper half of the paper leaving the lower fold still in place. Do not let the paper drop suddenly or it may tear.
Holding the top of the paper between fingers and thumb, position the top edge to overlap the ceiling or cornice by about 50mm. Slide the wallpaper into position, aligning the right-hand edge with the vertical guide line on the wall.

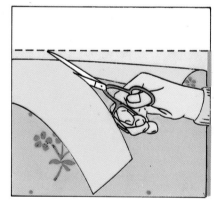

If necessary, add a little extra paste to the top edge first.
Trim the edge at skirting board level in the same way, and along the window frame if it overlaps.
Remove any paste from the ceiling or woodwork with a damp sponge.

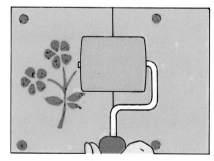

13 *Use a seam roller* △
To smooth the edges, go over the seams with a seam roller about 20 minutes after hanging. Do not roll embossed papers – dab seams firmly with the hanging brush instead.

Turning a corner ▷

Room corners are rarely square, so a length of paper that turns a corner should be hung as two strips. Measure the distance from the last length of paper to the corner in several places. For internal corners, add 15mm to the widest measurement; for external corners, such as round a chimney breast, add 35mm.

Cut a length of paper to this width and hang it with the cut edge brushed into (or around) the corner. Measure the width of the remainder of the paper and then measure this distance from the corner. Hang a plumb line from this point and mark the wall. Paste and hang the paper, overlapping the amount carried round – any slight pattern mismatch will not show.

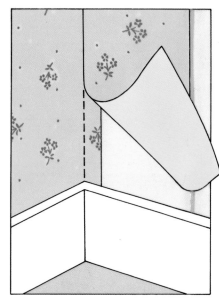

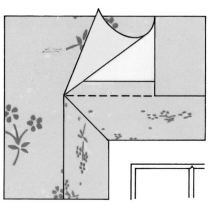

Paper a window recess △

Paper the inside of the recess first, turning a 15mm flap on to the surrounding wall. Then paper the wall round the window, cutting out the shape exactly.

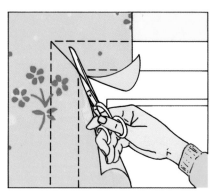

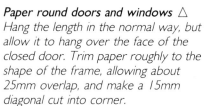

Paper round doors and windows △

Hang the length in the normal way, but allow it to hang over the face of the closed door. Trim paper roughly to the shape of the frame, allowing about 25mm overlap, and make a 15mm diagonal cut into corner.

Brush the paper into the angle between wall and frame, mark a crease line with the back of the scissors and trim.

If possible, centre short lengths over doors and windows with full lengths on either side.

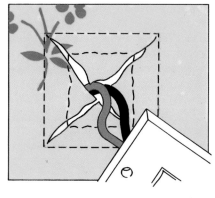

Paper round switches and sockets △

Paper straight over a light switch or socket, then use a sharp knife to make diagonal cuts to the corners (or several cuts if it is circular). Press the flaps back into position and trim the edges.

If the face plate is removable, turn off the electricity at the mains and then unscrew the plate. Instead of trimming off the flaps, simply tuck them behind the plate. Do not use this method with foil wallpaper.

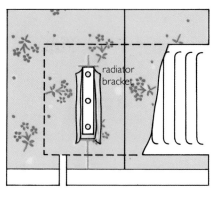

Paper round radiators △

Let the paper hang over the face of the radiator and cut a slit up from the bottom of the length so that the paper can pass either side of the radiator bracket. Then make 15mm horizontal slits at top and bottom of bracket. Tuck paper behind radiator and smooth around the bracket fixing.

BRIGHT IDEA

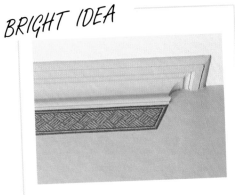

A NEAT EDGE

After decorating, hang a wallpaper border at ceiling level to tidy up edges. If a cornice ends with a sloping ceiling (in a stairwell, say) trim the border edge and paste it over the short end to highlight the angle.

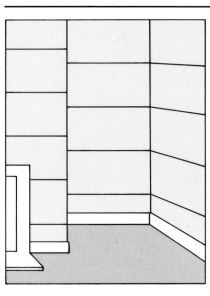

LINING PAPER

If lining paper is to be painted over, hang it vertically as for standard wallpaper.

If it is to be covered with another wallcovering, hang it horizontally to avoid vertical joins coinciding in the two layers. Use the same paste that will be used for the final wallcovering.

Start at ceiling level and work down, butting joins closely. Leave to dry for 24 hours. If edges do overlap, lightly rub them down with medium-grade abrasive paper.

DECORATING CEILINGS

Papering a ceiling can give a room an attractive new look as well as hiding fine cracks and uneven plaster.

Although papering a ceiling is not the easiest of jobs, there are far fewer obstructions to cope with than you'll find when papering the walls of a typical room. It is still, however, best tackled by two people – with one person supporting the weight of the paper while the other coaxes it into position. If you are papering a whole room, start with the ceiling and then paper the walls. If you are also putting up a ceiling rose (page 68), fix the rose after papering rather than having to paper round it.

Choosing wallpaper Steer clear of cheap, thin wallpaper that can stretch and tear easily when wet with paste.

Choose a medium-weight paper, either plain or with a small all-over design so that you don't have to worry about matching it up.

If the ceiling is in poor condition but you want a painted finish, a fine-textured paper is a good choice. Heavier relief and embossed papers are difficult to handle at ceiling height.

Preparation Prepare a ceiling for decorating as you would a plastered wall but don't worry about hairline cracks that will be hidden by the paper. If the ceiling is newly plastered, treat it with a generous coat of size (watered-down wallpaper paste).

Before you start to paper the ceiling, remove any light fittings.

Where to start papering It's traditional to work inwards from and parallel to the main window in the room so that any overlapping edges won't be highlighted. However, it may be easier to work at right angles to the window if this means that you'll be handling shorter, more manageable lengths of paper (in a long, thin room for example).

TOOLS AND EQUIPMENT

You need the same tool kit for papering a ceiling as you do for basic wall-papering (see Hanging Wallpaper, pages 61-64).

You may also need a screwdriver to take down ceiling lights: it's easier to do this than try to paper round them.

Access For safety and comfort, you need a strong platform which can be positioned at working height directly beneath each length. It's no good trying to perch on chairs or small steps.

All-over print
Pretty co-ordinating paper on the ceiling makes this room look cosy and intimate.

CHECK YOUR NEEDS

- ☐ Wallpaper
- ☐ Paste
- ☐ Steel tape and pencil
- ☐ String and coloured chalk
- ☐ Table for cutting and pasting
- ☐ Long-bladed scissors
- ☐ Small scissors or craft knife
- ☐ Plastic bucket for paste
- ☐ Pasting brush or 100mm paint brush
- ☐ Paper-hanging brush (or sponge for washables)
- ☐ Screwdriver
- ☐ Old rags or sponge
- ☐ Seam roller
- ☐ Stepladders, planks, etc.

HOW MANY ROLLS?

Estimate the number of rolls you need by measuring the distance round the walls of the room.

This chart is calculated for standard wallpaper which is sold in rolls approximately 10.05m long, 530mm wide.

Distance around the room (m)	10	11	12	13	14	15	16	17	18	19	20
No of rolls	2	2	2	3	3	4	4	4	5	5	5
Distance around the room (m)	21	22	23	24	25	26	27	28	29	30	
No of rolls	6	7	7	8	8	9	10	10	11	11	

Buy all wallpaper at the same time, checking that batch numbers are the same to avoid colour variations. If the paper has a large pattern repeat, buy an extra roll.

1 *Mark a guideline* ▷
Decide where you're going to start papering.

Then, at both ends of the wall you'll be working from, measure out across the ceiling a distance of 25mm less than the width of the paper to allow an overlap at the wall angle; mark with a pencil.

Coat a length of string with coloured chalk. Pin to the ceiling edges, aligned with the pencil marks, and snap it against the ceiling. Remove string.

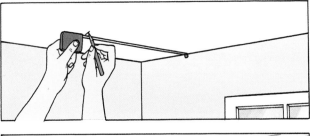

2 *Cut paper to size*
Measure from wall to wall and cut the first length, allowing an extra 100mm for trimming the paper at each end.

Cut all the other lengths too. If the paper has a pattern, match subsequent lengths with the previous one. Number and mark the backs so that the paper is hung in the right order and the pattern is always in the same direction.

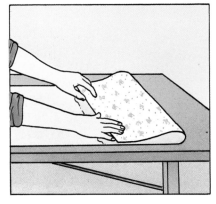

3 *Paste and fold* △
Mix up the wallpaper adhesive according to manufacturer's instructions. Then lay the first length face down on the table, and paste in the normal way but fold in a concertina fashion: paste an area almost as long as the table and fold this up into a series of pleats about 450mm wide, keeping the pasted side inside each fold.

Move the folded paper along the table, and paste and fold the rest of the paper in the same way. When you reach the far end of the length, turn the last fold back on itself to ensure that you don't get paste on to the front of the paper.

4 *Paste the ceiling* ▷
Some papers must be left for a few minutes for the paste to soak in or they'll wrinkle when hung – follow the instructions on the roll label. Lay this paper to one side and paste the next length in the meantime.

When you're ready to hang the paper, apply some adhesive to the ceiling itself at the start of each length of paper so that it won't come unstuck as you work along the ceiling.

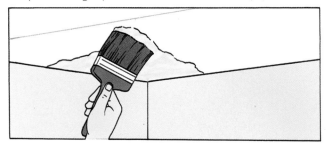

5 Hang the first length ▷

If you are working on your own, carefully pick up the pasted paper, using a roll of paper to support it in one hand while you brush the paper into place with the other.

To hang the first length, start in one corner, facing the wall you are working from. Peel back the last fold you made, line it up with the chalk line and brush the paper firmly into the angles between wall and ceiling. Remember to leave a trimming allowance.

Moving back along the work platform, gradually unfold the paper and brush out to remove any air bubbles. Make sure you hold the folded length as close to the ceiling as possible – this can be tiring but if you let your arm drop, the weight of the folds may drag the newly pasted paper away from the ceiling.

Working in pairs ▷

If you have a helper, one person can support the paper on a clean broom from floor-level while the other walks along the platform brushing it on to the ceiling. This makes papering much easier, and is far less tiring. Hang the paper in the same way as described above.

6 Trim the edges ▷

At short and long side edges, trim the paper so that it butts neatly up to wall or cornice. If there is no cornice or you will paper the walls next, allow a 10mm overlap.

To trim, crease paper into ceiling angle with the back of a scissor blade. Peel paper back, cut along crease, and brush back down. Finish by wiping off any smears of paste with a damp rag or sponge.

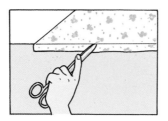

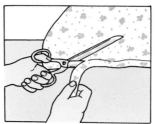

7 Hang the other lengths

Working away from the wall, hang subsequent lengths in exactly the same way as the first. Butt the edges neatly together, and match the pattern if any.

The last length will probably be less than a full-width. Measure and cut to size before pasting and hanging, allowing 25mm extra width for trimming the long side edge against the wall.

8 Use a seam roller

When all the lengths are hung, go over the seams with a seam roller to make sure that the edges of each length are well stuck down. Place a piece of paper under the roller so that it doesn't mark the newly pasted wallcovering.

Do not roll relief or embossed papers – dab the seams firmly with the ends of the hanging brush or a soft cloth instead.

CUTTING ROUND FITTINGS

Before starting to paper the ceiling, **turn off the electricity at the mains.** The main fuse box is usually found in an out of the way cupboard or corner of the kitchen or hall; the main switch will read OFF in large letters when the power is turned off.

Then remove light bulb and shade, unscrew the fitting cover and disconnect the pendant flex (make a colour drawing of the wiring first so that you can replace the flex correctly). To protect the wiring from wet paste, screw the fitting cover back on before papering over it.

1 Pierce the paper

Paper the ceiling as described above up to the light position. When you come to the fitting cover, press the paper lightly over it. Then pierce the paper directly beneath the cover with a sharp pair of scissors.

2 Cut and trim △

Make several cuts outwards from the hole to reveal the fitting cover. Partly unscrew the cover, brush the paper round it and trim until there is just enough left to tuck behind. Press the edges of the paper firmly on to the ceiling, then continue hanging the rest of the length. Finish by replacing the flex and fitting cover.

BRIGHT IDEA

CUT OUT AIR BUBBLES

Use a sharp knife or razor blade to cut a neat cross in any bubbles that are still there a couple of days after papering.

Fold back the corners of the cuts, dab some paste behind, then smooth the flaps back and press firmly into position. Wipe off any excess paste with a damp sponge or rag.

DECORATIVE CEILING ROSES

A ceiling rose is a flat, circular centre-piece, often used with a suspended light fitting. The steps below cover fixing a rose with a back recess for fitting over electrical connections.

Buying a ceiling rose Ceiling roses come in a wide range of sizes and designs. Most are made from traditional fibrous plaster or from cheaper plastic materials such as polystyrene and polyurethane. Plaster types are heavy: they must be nailed or screwed to the joists above the ceiling as well as stuck into position. Plastic types are light and can be glued to the ceiling, although it's best to use panel pins as well for extra support. Always use adhesive and fixings recommended by the manufacturer.

1 Find the room centre
Except in long rooms where two roses may be fitted, it's usual to fit the rose in the centre of the ceiling. If there isn't already a light fitting at this point, stretch two strings diagonally across the ceiling from corner to corner; where they intersect is the centre point.

2 Adapt the ceiling rose
If the rose is to be used with an existing pendant light, you may have to drill a hole through the middle of it to take the flex (some roses come with a hole ready drilled). Turn off the electricity at the mains, and remove the bulb, lampholder and shade or, if necessary, the fitting cover.

Relief detail △
Here, the decorative mouldings are picked out in apricot, while the ceiling is painted a paler shade of the same colour. See below for how to fix a rose with a heavy fitting.

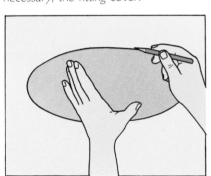

3 Prepare the ceiling △
Cut a paper template which is slightly smaller than the rose and use it to mark off the area to be prepared. If the ceiling is painted, lightly rub down with abrasive paper so that the adhesive will get a good grip. Any wallpaper should be stripped. If you've just papered, cut round the marked area with a sharp knife and peel the paper away. If the paper is old, try to strip it dry – only soak if necessary as you may damage surrounding paper.

If fixing a plaster rose, knock or probe the ceiling with a bradawl to find the joists and mark the positions.

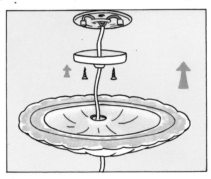

4 Fix the ceiling rose △
Spread a layer of adhesive all round the outer rim on the back of the rose with a filling knife. Feed the flex through the hole in the rose (replacing the fitting cover if it has been removed). Then press the rose firmly into position; wipe off any adhesive that squeezes out with a damp sponge.

For extra support, drive panel pins in at an angle through the face of a plastic type rose – three or four pins should be sufficient. Fix a plaster rose to the ceiling joists with rust-proof nails or screws, then fill in the holes with ordinary all-purpose filler.

5 Paint the rose
Paint the rose the same colour as walls or ceiling, or accentuate the decoration by picking out the relief details in a contrasting colour. A matt or silky finish looks better than gloss, while a water-based emulsion is less likely to clog up the mouldings than an oil-based paint. Apply two coats of paint with a small artist's brush.

Replace lampholder, bulb and shade.

FIXING HEAVY FITTINGS

When fixing a heavy light fitting:
☐ unscrew and remove the base plate, and disconnect the flex
☐ mark the rose and drill holes for the flex and screws that support the light fitting.
☐ apply adhesive, thread flex through centre hole and re-connect wires. Press into position
☐ replace the light, screwing the fitting's baseplate through the rose into the joist.

HANGING RELIEF WALLCOVERINGS

Relief decorations give walls and ceilings an attractive, textured finish, and help to disguise poor surfaces.

If you want to decorate your walls and ceilings with plain colour rather than pattern, but you fancy a surface with texture instead of the smoothness of painted plaster, then relief decorations may be the answer. They provide a surface embossed with a pattern that may be regular or random, and are designed to be painted over once they have been hung, giving a relatively permanent finish. There are several qualities and weights to choose from.

LOW-RELIEF PAPER
The least expensive type is known as low-relief or dry-embossed paper, or by Crown's trade name, Anaglypta Original (now often used as a generic term). It consists of two layers of paper bonded together with adhesive and embossed by passing it between steel rollers while the adhesive is still wet. Anaglypta is hung with an all-purpose adhesive, and care must be taken not to fill the hollows on the back of the paper or overstretching will occur. It's important to let the paste soak into the paper after it has been pasted so it becomes supple and easier to hang; the manufacturers will recommend a time, but 10 minutes is about average.

HIGH-RELIEF PAPER
Deep-embossed papers, such as Anaglypta Supadurable, are more expensive than Anaglypta Original, but are stronger and heavier. They're not actually paper at all, since they're made from cotton fibres rather than wood pulp, and can take a far deeper emboss than Anaglypta Original.

The design is moulded into the paper while it is still wet, which ensures that the embossing is retained after pasting and hanging. This means that these papers are much easier for the amateur to handle. (With some of the more

▷ **Glowing colours**
A rich red painted finish is a traditional choice for this Edwardian style Lincrusta dado. Gloss paint emphasizes the heavy moulding as light catches on the raised areas.

heavily-embossed Anaglypta Original-type wallcoverings the relief tends to flatten unless great care is taken during the hanging process.) Again, an all-purpose adhesive containing a fungicide should be used, and each length should be soaked for the time the manufacturer recommends.

BLOWN VINYLS
Blown vinyl wallcoverings are made from a moulded layer of vinyl bonded to a paper backing; Anaglypta Luxury Vinyl and Anaglypta Fine Vinyl are good examples of this type of wallcovering. The vinyl layer is heated during manufacture to make it expand slightly, giving the raised parts a spongy texture.

Because it is blown rather than embossed, and has a paper backing, there are no hollows on the back; this makes pasting easier, and there is no need to soak the length before hanging it. Ready-pasted types are available, otherwise use an all-purpose paste containing a fungicide. Stripping blown vinyls is much easier than stripping other

relief papers, because the vinyl surface layer is peeled from the paper backing like an ordinary vinyl wallcovering.

LINCRUSTA
Lincrusta is a heavy, solid embossed wallcovering made from oxidized linseed oil and fillers bonded to a paper backing; it was first manufactured in the late 19th century. It is intended primarily for use on the dado (below the chair rail) particularly in hallways, as it gives such a durable finish.

The linoleum-like surface is embossed while it is still soft, and is then allowed to dry out and harden for about 14 days. The result is an immensely durable wallcovering with a high relief which can be redecorated almost indefinitely. This is just as well, since getting it off again can be extremely difficult. It is hung with a special adhesive called Lincrusta glue. Most types have a selvedge which has to be trimmed off before hanging.

DIMENSIONS AND FINISHES
All these relief wallcoverings come in standard-sized rolls measuring 10.05m (33ft) long and about 520mm (20½in) wide, although some Lincrustas are made in narrower widths as well for ease of handling. Lincrusta is also available in panels of various sizes.

Most relief wallcoverings can be painted with either emulsion or oil-based paints (eggshell finish or high gloss). Lincrusta should only be painted with an oil-based paint, and looks most effective decorated with an oil-based glaze tinted with colour.

SURFACE PREPARATION

If you are planning to hang relief decorations over bare plaster or painted walls, they should be thoroughly washed down and sized. However, old wallcoverings and lining paper should always be stripped off (see Preparing Walls). With Lincrusta, care must be taken to remove any flaky paint before hanging lining paper, since the adhesive is likely to pull this away.

It's a good idea to hang lining paper before putting up any type of relief decoration, as this provides a uniformly absorbent surface on new or repaired plasterwork, and helps the paste to dry out on non-absorbent painted surfaces. Hang the lining paper horizontally on walls and, on ceilings, at right angles to the final paper direction. Use paste containing a fungicide if you're hanging blown vinyl paper or Lincrusta. For more details, see Hanging Wallpaper and Decorating Ceilings, pages 61–68.

HANGING LINCRUSTA

1 Prepare the walls △
Start by preparing the walls: old wallcoverings should be removed, paint washed down and cracks made good. All flaky paint should be removed. Since Lincrusta is difficult to trim to fit into awkward corners, it is a good idea to fit new skirting boards and dado (or picture) rails to give neat, smooth edges to butt the Lincrusta to. Walls should be cross lined (papered horizontally with lining paper) to give an evenly porous surface.

2 Cut the drops △
Always handle Lincrusta with care to avoid damaging or cracking its surface. Start by cutting lengths to fit the area to be covered: they should be 50mm longer than the longest drop. Ensure that the pattern matches on each drop. Trim the selvedge, using a sharp craft knife and a steel straight-edge; it's easiest to do this on the floor, with a sheet of hardboard underneath the edges being trimmed. Undercut the selvedges slightly by angling the knife blade inwards to ensure perfect joins.

3 Soak the backing △
Sponge the paper backing of each length with warm water, and leave it flat to soak for 20 to 30 minutes. Place the lengths back to back in pairs for the best results. This helps the material to expand fully before hanging, and so prevents blisters forming when the lengths are hung. After the soaking period, wipe off any surplus water with a dry cloth.

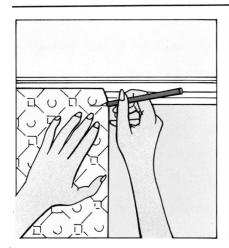

4 Get it straight △
Use the plumb bob and line to plumb a line on the wall surface at your starting point, and hold the first length up before pasting so you can mark the cutting line at each side. Then trim through the two marks to get a perfect fit at the dado rail, picture rail or ceiling level; leave the bottom edge of the length for trimming after hanging.

5 Cut round obstructions △
If there are other obstructions such as light switches and window openings, get a helper to hold the length in place while you mark their positions. If the obstruction is close to the edge of the paper this can be done freehand. Otherwise, measure the position of the obstruction and mark on the Lincrusta. Cut out as marked.

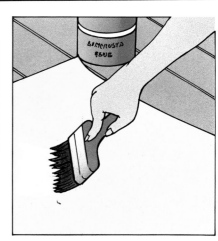

6 Paste the Lincrusta △
Brush the Lincrusta glue on to the back of the first length using an old 75mm wide paint brush.
If the glue is too thick to spread easily, stir it vigorously. Make sure that the whole surface is evenly covered and pay particular attention to the edges.

7 Hang the first drop
Hang the length immediately pasting is complete, aligning the trimmed top edge with the dado rail, picture rail or ceiling line and one side edge with your plumbed line. Press it into position with a warm wet cloth, working from top to bottom.

Keep the edge level with the plumbed line, and be careful not to bend the Lincrusta at the lower edge. Continue until the Lincrusta is stuck in position to about 20cm above the skirting.

8 Trim the bottom edge ▷
At the bottom of the length, mark the level of the skirting board at each side. Then place a strip of hardboard against the wall behind the bottom edge and cut through the two marks using your knife and straightedge. Press the bottom edge back into place on the wall.

Wipe off surplus adhesive from paintwork or the surface of the Lincrusta with a sponge as you hang each length. Hang subsequent lengths in the same way, butt-joining the lengths as accurately as possible.

9 Dealing with corners
Because of its thickness, Lincrusta is very difficult to hang round corners unless they are fairly well rounded. It may be possible with some thinner types, depending on the design, but it is generally better with sharp corners to cut the length that turns the corner and to butt-join the two sections to obtain a neater finish.

10 Finishing the job
Leave the Lincrusta to dry out for at least 24 hours, and preferably for a couple of days. Then wipe the surface down with a clean cloth dipped in white spirit to remove any greasy finger marks or dirt that could spoil the paint finish.

BRIGHT IDEA

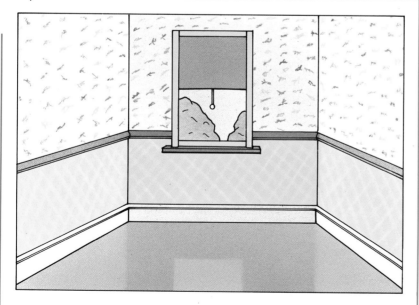

Childproof walls In children's rooms, it is the lower metre of the walls which gets most wear and tear (with experiments with crayons, sticky fingers and so on). To protect the walls as much as possible, put up a dado rail and hang a heavily embossed or blown vinyl paper on the dado. Then paint with gloss paint.

This means that you can re-paint the lower part of the wall when necessary without having to go to the trouble of re-decorating the whole room.

DECORATING RELIEF WALLCOVERINGS
You can decorate relief wallcoverings with any good quality paint, but Lincrusta should be painted with an oil-based (eggshell or gloss) paint. For a sheen finish, which emphasises the texture of the wallcovering, use eggshell, or choose gloss for a tougher finish.

However, for a more interesting finish, you could apply a scumbled finish: scumbling is a technique which leaves colour mainly in the recesses of the surface and so helps to enhance its three dimensional look.

Scumble is a transparent oil glaze to which white spirit and various tints are added to produce a semi-transparent finish. Alternatively, the glaze can be coloured with artists' oil colours or any ordinary oil-based paint, such as eggshell or gloss.

Make up enough to complete the job, since colour-matching extra batches could be difficult. Prime the surface with a coat of oil-based eggshell paint and allow to dry before scumbling. Choose a colour several shades lighter than the glaze. The glaze should be thinned before use with a little white spirit to make it easier to apply.

Before starting work on the wall itself, it's a good idea to practise the technique on some offcuts so you can get a feel for how much glaze to apply and how much pressure to use to wipe it off again and achieve the desired effect. Work with a friend, one of you applying the scumble, the other wiping it off, to speed things up, so the glaze doesn't dry in patches.

APPLYING SCUMBLE

1 Brushing on the glaze
Start by brushing the glaze on to an area of about 1 sq m. Brush it well into the design to ensure an even coating, but not too thickly or it will run.

2 Wiping off ▷
Use a clean, dry, lint-free and colourfast cotton cloth, folded into a pad, to wipe the scumble off the high spots. Wipe lightly then increase the pressure to get the effect you want. Finish by wiping downwards.

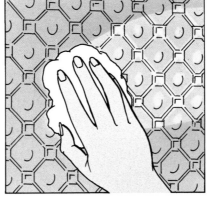

3 Move to the next section
Repeat the process for subsequent sections, trying to keep a wet edge going so the joins do not show. Remember that the final wipe should be downwards on each section to ensure a matching finish.

4 Protect the surface
Leave the scumbled surface to dry for about 24 hours. Then apply a coat of clear varnish – satin gives a softer finish than gloss – to protect the surface and make it completely washable.

◁ Out of the shadows
The scumbling technique shows up clearly here: you can see how the greatest depth of colour collects in the recesses of the blown vinyl wallcovering. The grey-blue shade chosen gives the wall an almost metallic sheen.

▷ Hall stories
Two different patterns of Anaglypta Original have been used to great effect in this hallway. Below the dado rail, the pattern has been painted in a silk finish paint to match the woodwork. Above the rail, a border pattern has been painted to match the wall above. The border pattern is particularly effective when used on the ceiling to imitate a cornice.

WALLCOVERINGS

Wallcoverings used to be available just in paper, now you can choose from many different materials, types and textures.

CHECKLIST
☐ Most rolls of wallcovering are 10.05m long and 530mm wide.
☐ If using a patterned wallcovering check how far apart the pattern repeat is; the larger the pattern, the more waste has to be allowed for.
☐ The wallcovering's wrapper should tell you if it can be washed, scrubbed or sponged, or if it is ready-pasted.
☐ Although wallpapers are hung with standard wallpaper paste, many other sorts of wallcoverings require a special adhesive. Ask your retailer for advice.

Once you have decided to cover the walls of your home with a wallcovering, there are certain decisions to take before going shopping.

The type that you choose must be right for the room in which it is to go: kitchens and bathrooms need something to stand up to steam and condensation; landings and hallways, or rooms with several doors leading off them, receive most wear and tear, so cover these walls with a fairly hardwearing wallcovering. Dining area and kitchen walls are most likely to become stained with food, so a washable or spongeable wallcovering is ideal.

The state of the walls If the plaster is old and bumpy a thick relief or textured paper conceals the faults. Thin papers are best on newer, smoother surfaces. An all-over pattern also helps to hide defects by distracting the eye.

The cost Prices vary from the cheapest wallpaper to the most expensive natural fabric wallcovering. Decide whether you want something that is going to last, in which case an expensive wallcovering is money well spent; or whether you may want a change in a year or two, in which case look at cheaper papers.

WALLCOVERING GROUPS

WHITES
These are designed to be painted over after hanging. They then become semi-permanent, as future decorating need only consist of a fresh coat of paint each time.

Relief paper This type of paper has a pattern embossed in it to give a raised effect on the surface. Anaglypta is a typical example, it comes in relief patterns ranging from weaves to florals. Superdurable is a much thicker paper made with cotton fibres to give it more pronounced relief.

It's important to let the paste soak into relief paper so it becomes supple and easier to hang but care must be taken not to fill the hollows on the back or stretching will occur.

Lincrusta is a rather different type of relief wallcovering. It is very thick and heavyweight, made from linseed oil and fillers mounted on a backing paper. It is deeply embossed, usually with a pattern echoing the period when it was invented – the Edwardian era. It is expensive but durable and must be hung with special adhesive.

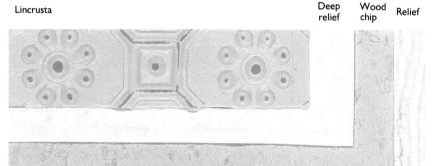

Lincrusta   Deep relief   Wood chip   Relief

Woodchip paper Also known as ingrain paper, it consists of wood particles sandwiched between two thin sheets of paper, giving a lumpy, porridge-like surface. It is ideal for covering bad plaster. Better grades are white, and can be left for a time without painting; but they soon start to yellow.

Lining paper (not shown), is a thin paper which should be hung to line walls before hanging expensive or heavyweight wallcoverings, or if the walls are rough and uneven. For lining purposes it should be hung horizontally.

PRINTED PAPERS
This is by far the largest group of wallcoverings. It includes all the papers available that are printed in thousands of patterns and colourways. Depending on what you choose, the price range is as wide as the choice of designs.

Machine-printed wallpapers. The pattern and design on this type is printed by machine. The price reflects the thickness of the paper and the number of different colours used. The pattern or design can either be simply printed on the surface of the paper or stamped into it too to give an embossed or textured effect.

Hand-printed wallpapers offer superb designs and colours, but they are usually much more expensive than machine-printed papers. The colours can sometimes smear if wetted by paste, and because hand-printing is not as accurate as machine printing, getting a pattern to match between two lengths can be tricky.

Sometimes the plain paper edging down each side of the roll is left untrimmed by the manufacturer, although most reputable specialist shops trim them for you before selling them.

Machine-printed   Hand-printed

PVC coated (not shown) Many printed papers are coated with a thin layer of plastic to make them washable or spongeable. The thicker the coating, the more it repels water, so the thinnest coatings are only spongeable. However, even those with the thickest plastic coating should not be scrubbed as this can damage the coating.

Remember that as they repel water they can be very hard to strip, so make sure when buying that you choose one which is dry-strippable (which means the paper can be stripped off the wall without soaking with water first).

VINYL WALLCOVERINGS

The design on this group of wallcoverings is not printed directly on to a roll of paper, but on to a thin layer of vinyl, which is then fused to a paper backing.

Although usually more expensive than wallpaper, vinyls are very popular, because they are not only washable but often scrubbable too.

Many vinyls are ready-pasted: the back is coated with dry paste which is activated when lengths are dipped in a trough of water. This makes hanging easy and does away with messy paste, pasting table and brush.

If the type you buy is not ready-pasted, be sure to paste it with fungicidal adhesive. Vinyl is non-porous, so it doesn't allow the wall behind it to breathe. This means any moisture in the wall is trapped and the wall or paper may go mouldy.

Vinyl can be stripped dry, so if you want to take it down you simply peel away the decorative vinyl layer, leaving the paper backing behind. This makes a good foundation for a wallcovering.
Standard vinyls are perfect if you want a printed wallcovering which is going to last longer and

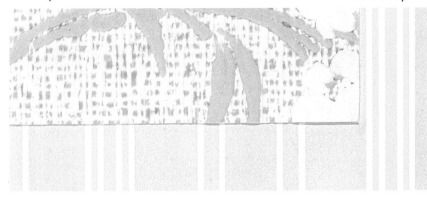

Blown vinyl   Standard vinyl

stand up to more wear and tear than ordinary wallpaper. There are thousands of designs and colours available as well as different effects.
Blown vinyls A blown vinyl is produced by a heat process which makes the vinyl expand to give a blown, raised effect. The first blown vinyls were

produced in off-white shades designed for overpainting, so they could also be grouped under 'whites'. But coloured and patterned ones are now proving very popular. Although a blown vinyl has a raised effect the backing layer remains flat, so it is much easier to paste and hang.

FABRICS AND NATURAL MATERIALS

Many printed and embossed wallcoverings imitate fabrics, textiles and natural materials, but it is possible to hang the real thing, although it tends to be more expensive.

An unbacked fabric wallcovering is wider than a standard wallcovering width and designed to be hung on walls by stretching it round partitions or backing panels first and then mounting these onto your walls. (You are really only likely to need unbacked fabric if you have very uneven walls, such as those found in old houses and cottages).

By far the easiest way of hanging fabric on your walls is to buy a fabric wallcovering that is backed with either paper, plastic or latex. These are much more expensive than ordinary wallpapers. They usually come in standard widths and should be hung with special adhesives. (Ask your retailer for advice on which adhesive is suitable).
Cork A cork wallcovering is made from thin sheets of real bark from the cork oak tree, glued onto a paper backing. The cork is available in its natural colours or dyed. The swirling grain of the bark gives each piece a unique natural pattern.

Cork, however, is prone to crumbling so it is

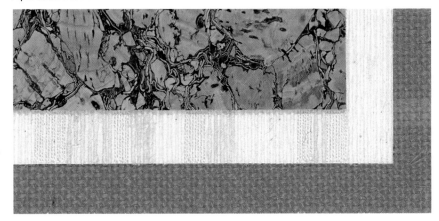

Paper-backed cork   Textile   Hessian

not terribly easy to hang nor is it that suitable to hang on walls which are likely to receive a lot of wear and tear.
Hessian is one of the most popular fabric wallcoverings if you want to create a rustic look. It is available in a range of colours and comes paper-

or latex-backed.
Other textiles There are many other paper or vinyl-backed woven textile wallcoverings ranging from real silk and wool to synthetic fibres. Look out for those which are coated in vinyl and therefore washable.

SPECIAL EFFECTS

This group covers other types of wallcoverings not already mentioned, because they are unique in the way they look and the methods by which they are made.
Foil wallcoverings consist of a thin layer of metallized plastic film on a paper backing. They reflect every speck of light to create a shiny mirror effect. They can be machine- or hand-printed and must be hung with a special adhesive. They are expensive, but ideal for small areas that receive little natural light. They should be hung only on flat walls, as the slightest dent or bump shows up. Metal foil conducts electricity and so should not be tucked behind light switches.
Foam polyethylene This decorative wallcovering is unlike any other. The design is printed on to foamed plastic, which is lightweight and therefore easy to hang.

The paste is applied to the wall, not the wallcovering, either with a paint roller or large brush, and the wallcovering is hung straight from the roll – there is no need to cut it to length first.

It is warm to the touch and, unlike vinyl, allows the wall behind to breathe. This makes it a good choice for kitchens or bathrooms where condensation is a problem. Its light weight makes it easy to hang in stairwells and on ceilings. Like

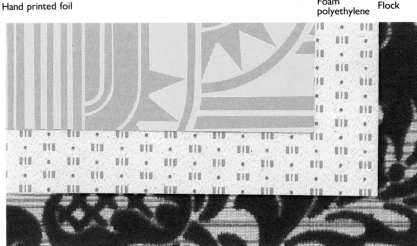

Hand printed foil   Foam polyethylene   Flock

vinyls it is washable and dry-strippable, but not as tough.
Flock This has the luxurious look and feel of velvet. The rich pile is produced not by weaving but by gluing short lengths of silk or other fibres to a paper backing, then cutting a design into it. The

designs are usually traditional Victorian and Edwardian formalized florals or stripes, in rich red, green and gold colours. Traditional flocks are hard to hang as paste smears ruin the pile; but vinyl versions are easier and may even come ready-pasted. Both should be brushed regularly.

CORNICES AND COVINGS

A cornice adds the finishing touch to any room, and hides unsightly gaps between the walls and ceiling.

A cornice is any continuous length of horizontal moulding between walls and ceiling. Coving is the name given to the pre-fabricated moulding used to make a cornice. Traditional cornices are often elaborate and richly embossed. Modern cornices are usually a simple length of concave coving.

As well as providing a decorative break between the walls and ceiling, and hiding gaps, a cornice can also be used to conceal pipework and wiring.

HOW CORNICES ARE MADE

Cornices can be made from plaster or wood, expanded plastic foam, plasterboard or polystyrene (the last three materials are sold under the name coving).

Plaster Elaborate cornices found in period homes are usually made from moulded plaster. It is possible to buy new lengths of plaster coving but the material is difficult and heavy to work with and expensive.

Wood Some traditional carved cornices are made from wood, either painted or stained. It is difficult to replace this type of cornice without using the services of an expert woodcarver. You can add a simple wooden cornice to a room using lengths of scotia moulding.

Expanded plastic foam If a traditional plaster cornice is very badly damaged, it may be possible to replace it with a reproduction design made in rigid expanded plastic foam. The material has a lightweight core, a hard, smooth surface, and comes in many styles. It is light in weight, easy to fit and can be cut, drilled and sanded. The more elaborate the design, the more this type of cornice costs but even the most expensive designs are cheaper than the same

Period elegance
A carefully restored cornice adds a touch of authentic elegance to this cool blue living room. A similar effect can be achieved with modern reproduction coving.

thing in plaster. This type of cornice can be left unpainted, or coloured to match the room scheme.

Plasterboard Plasterboard coving can be used to make a simple cornice. It has a plaster core sheathed in a thick paper skin. It comes only as a plain concave quadrant with a hollow back, is fairly heavy and has no surface detail. It needs painting after fitting.

Polystyrene Available in a similar style to plasterboard coving, polystyrene is light in weight and has a slightly textured surface. It is easy to fit, comes with separate pre-formed internal and external mitre pieces and is inexpensive. It must be painted after fitting.

MEASURING UP

Coving for use in adding or replacing a cornice is sold in lengths – usually of 2 or 3m. Heavy plaster cornice is sold in short lengths or is made specially to measure.

Begin by finding out the lengths the coving you have chosen comes in then measure up the perimeter of the room and work out how many pieces will be needed. Remember that you have to cut corner mitre joints in most types which will entail some wastage.

SURFACE PREPARATION

Unless you are using anything but lightweight polystyrene coving, you will need to strip wallpaper from the area of wall and ceiling where the coving will fit. If this is not done the coving could fall down. If the wall is painted, wash it down and rub the area where the coving is to be fitted with sandpaper to provide a key for the adhesive.

TOOLS AND EQUIPMENT

Cutting Use a saw for plaster, plasterboard, expanded plastic foam and wood and a craft knife for polystyrene.
Measuring Equip yourself with a metal rule. If you are using plasterboard, plaster, wood or expanded plastic foam, you will need a mitre box. For small mouldings, use an ordinary carpenter's mitre box. For larger types, make a box, (see Step 5).

Fixing For lightweight coving, use the adhesive recommended by the maker. If the design is a heavy plaster moulded type, you will need masonry pins, wall plugs and screws, or frame plugs. This is a job for two, working from two pairs of step ladders with a plank across.

CHECK YOUR NEEDS

☐ Tape measure
☐ Metal rule and pencil
☐ Craft knife or saw
☐ Wallpaper scraper
☐ Mitre box
☐ Adhesive and adhesive spreader
☐ Filling knife
☐ Masonry pins, screws and wallplugs or frame plugs, plus drill, screwdriver or hammer for heavy types.
☐ Emulsion paint and brush

1 Make a guideline ▽
Using a length of coving held into the wall/ceiling angle as a guide, mark a guideline all around the room. Use a soft pencil to make the mark. This will help you to align the coving as you fix it and also indicates the area of old wallcovering to be stripped if the walls or ceilings are papered.

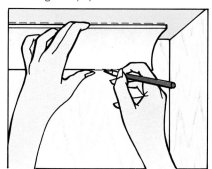

2 Mark the surface ▽
If paper has to be stripped, go over these lines with a metal rule and craft knife, cutting through into the plaster beneath. This will make a distinct line but don't worry as it will be covered once the cornice is in place. Keep the line as straight as possible and don't dig in too hard with the knife.

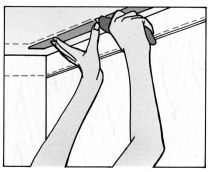

3 Strip the paper ▽
Dry-strip as much of the paper as you can from the wall and ceiling surfaces between the lines, by lifting seams between lengths. Don't soak it unless you have to, since you risk damaging the wallcovering further down the wall. It doesn't matter if some paper or old adhesive remains on the surface.

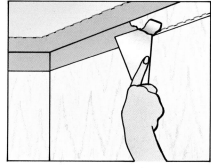

4 Painted surfaces
If the wall is painted, wash it down using a solution of sugar soap in water (follow manufacturer's instructions) to remove surface grease and dirt. Don't use too much water on the wall or it will run down and mark the paintwork below the ruled area. Leave the wall to dry then sand down between the marked lines with medium grade sandpaper, or with an electric sander. This will roughen the surface and provide a key for the adhesive. Wash down to remove loose dust and leave the wall to dry. If you try and fix coving to a damp or dusty wall the adhesive will not cling.

5 Make a mitre box ▷
If you are using large or ornate coving, time can be saved and mistakes avoided by making a mitre box to match the coving size. Make it about 450mm long, from wood about 19mm thick which is glued and screwed together and wide enough so the coving sits in the box just as it will in the floor/ceiling angle, with the edge of the coving that will rest upon the ceiling resting squarely on the base and the wall face against the box sides nearest you. Use a protractor to mark two saw guides at an angle of 45° facing in opposite directions. Cut them right down to the base of the box.

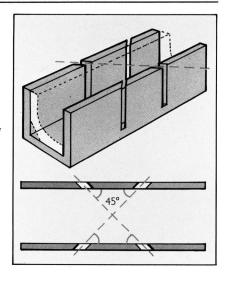

6 Measuring and cutting
Start at a corner. Unless mitres are ready cut you'll need to cut your own. The way the mitre is cut – from right to left, or left to right – depends on whether the corner is external or internal and which side of the mitre you are cutting (see Step 11). To cut the mitre correctly make two templates using offcuts of coving. Mark which face is to go against ceiling. Mitre one piece in the mitre box at one end, cutting from left to right. Make a parallel cut at other end. Mitre both ends of second piece but this time from right to left. When mitring the coving, put the templates in the appropriate corner to see which way to cut. When cutting mitres for external corners, the coving must be a bit longer than the wall.

7 Fitting the first piece ▽
Spread adhesive on to the back face of the first length. Hold in position on the wall and ceiling, checking that the edges are aligned with your guide line, and press firmly into position. Hold in place for a couple of minutes to give the adhesive a chance to grip.

8 Extra fixings ▽
For heavy coving, drive in masonry pins at 600mm intervals. For plaster coving position the coving, drill through into the wall and insert frame plugs (long wallplugs with a screw through the centre, which are pushed into the coving and screwed into the wall).

9 Make a neat finish ▷
When the length is firmly in position, use your filling knife to remove any excess adhesive that has squeezed out along the edges of the length of coving. This should automatically fill any gaps between the wall or ceiling and the edge of the coving caused by uneven surfaces. When using the filling knife, be careful not to mark the edge of the cornice or the wall or ceiling. If there are any gaps too wide to be covered by the adhesive fill them with a fine grade interior filler and smooth neatly. The filler can be sanded down for a fault-free finish.

10 Fitting the next length
Now mitre and fit a second length at the other end of the same wall. If the two lengths are longer than the wall, hold the second length in place after cutting the mitre on one end and mark the point at which it overlaps the second length. Make a straight square ended cut at this point, then apply adhesive and press the length into place. Use adhesive to fill the joint between the two lengths. Wipe off any smears. If the wall is longer than two lengths of coving, simply fill in the gap between the first and second lengths with one or more square-ended lengths as necessary.

11 Dealing with corners
Where two internal corner pieces meet, you may find it easier to push adhesive into the join with your finger or using a small piece of wood. It is important to get enough adhesive on the corner pieces to make a gap-free joint. All corner joints should be finished off neatly with a filling knife to make a good sharp join. This is important on external corners as gaps are most noticeable here. Wipe surplus adhesive away from the corners before it sets using a damp brush or a sponge.

12 Moving round the room
The diagram below left shows how coving is cut to fit a typical room. If possible, avoid having a short piece in the centre of a chimney breast. If short pieces are needed on other walls, they should be centred between long lengths.

CLEANING AND RESTORATION
In older homes it is common to find a beautifully moulded cornice so thick with paint that the detail has almost disappeared. It is possible to restore the cornice – providing that you have the time and the patience to embark on a painstaking paint stripping operation.
Identify the problem Start by trying to identify the paint used. If the surface is glossy, it's probably oil-based gloss paint. If the surface is matt and chalky, it may be either water-based distemper or oil based eggshell paint. If the surface is matt but sound, a modern emulsion paint has probably been used for the top coat.
Gloss and eggshell paint Either can be removed using paste or a gel stripper. If

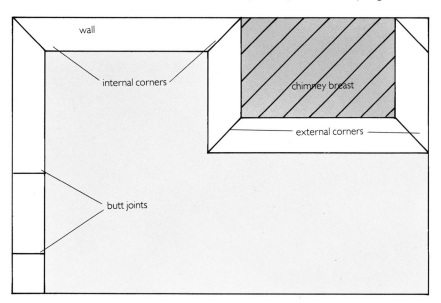

wall

internal corners

chimney breast

external corners

butt joints

using gel stripper, wear gloves and goggles as it burns skin if spilled. You can use a hot air stripper but it is rather tiring to hold the gun and work a scraper on cornice as you are constantly reaching upwards.

Distemper Try water first. If the surface is water-based distemper it will scrape away. Use a plant spray gun to keep the surface wet as you work (see right).

Emulsion paint This needs a chemical stripper. Some paint strippers won't work on emulsion so be sure to choose one which will (the instructions on the back of the can or packet will tell you).

Work slowly This is back-breaking work, so plan to do the job over several days. Remember that you may come across any combination of these paint types, so you will have to be prepared to switch your methods.

REPAIRING DAMAGE
You may find localized damage to the plaster moulding as you remove the paint. Patch or restore this using a quick-setting material such as alabastine or plaster of Paris. If large sections of detail are missing, make a mould using an undamaged area as your model. The best material for mould making is dental impression compound, which is available from dental materials suppliers (see Yellow Pages for firms in your area). Spread the inside of the mould with silicone grease and use quick-setting filler to form the new piece. When set, stick in place with epoxy-resin adhesive.

PAINTING THE CORNICE
Once the cornice is in place or stripped, it can be painted. Use emulsion, thinning the first coat on plaster and plasterboard with about 10 per cent extra water. Add a second coat when the first coat is dry. To avoid filling in the detail on ornate types, apply two thin coats rather than one thick one.

You may decide to redecorate ornate coving using coloured paint to pick out detail. Apply overall background colour as described. Apply colour using a small artist's brush, supported on a mahlstick – a 460mm length of dowelling with a small ball of foam wrapped in cloth at the end (see right). This helps to steady your hand. The small test pots of emulsion sold by the major paint manufacturers are ideal.

An eye for detail
Using simple modern coving to create a cornice adds the essential finishing touch to this room. The cornice and skirting are painted cream to contrast with the blue colour scheme and to match the furniture.

BRIGHT IDEA

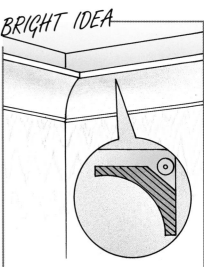

Hidden fittings Most modern covings are hollow at the back allowing you to conceal wiring. Make sure the coving you buy will fit over whatever you are trying to conceal. A variation on this idea is to use coving to hide slimline fluorescent tubes which beam up to the ceiling. The coving is positioned about 75mm down from the ceiling and only attached to the walls. This leaves a space for the light to shine upwards and for tubes to be replaced. Specially-made coving is available from lighting specialists.

FIXING FABRIC TO WALLS

Fabric-lined walls give a luxurious air to living rooms and bedrooms and can disguise damaged walls.

If you want to create warmth and softness in a room, fabric-lined walls may well be the answer. In a similar way to tongued-and-grooved cladding, fabric can be used to cover up poor plasterwork, and for real warmth you can add insulation under the fabric. However, it can be a fairly expensive business as fabric costs more per square metre than most wallcoverings, and for the technique described here, with fabric gathered on to curtain rods, the gathering means you will need even more fabric.

Slotting fabric on to rods means that you can actually take the fabric down for cleaning from time to time. It does involve a fair amount of sewing, particularly if you want to add a frill in a contrasting colour.

CHOOSE YOUR FABRICS

Plain fabrics or small patterns give the best effects when covering walls. Large patterns can be overpowering, and you have to be very careful to match up the motifs when joining widths. Pleat the fabric in your hands before buying to test the effect. Go for fabrics which are as wide and cheap as possible; but avoid ones which fade (eg dressmaking fabrics) if the room gets direct sunlight.

Calculating fabric quantities To calculate fabric quantities you will need to draw a sketch of each wall to be covered. Divide the walls into rectangular areas, with each rectangle as large as possible.

For example, on a wall with a pair of windows, you will have floor to ceiling rectangles on either side and between the windows, with smaller rectangles above and below the windows. For each rectangle you will need a panel of fabric at least one-and-a-half times the width, and measuring the height of the rectangle plus 8cm for casings top and bottom.

TOOLS AND EQUIPMENT

For fabric slotted on to curtain rods you will need enough rods to run all the way across the upper and lower edge of each rectangle. If the plasterwork is bad, or if your walls are difficult to fix into, you will find it easier to fit timber battens up before fixing the curtain rod brackets. Use 12mm diameter metal curtain rod; or, as a cheaper alternative, curtain wires held with screw eyes fixed to battens.

Note Radiators create problems: if you can remove them, fit the fabric behind, then replace the radiators, slitting the fabric where the brackets are positioned. If not, box them in beforehand. Take this into account when measuring up and deciding where to fix battens and curtain rods.

CHECK YOUR NEEDS
- [ ] 50×25mm battens (optional)
- [ ] Screws and wallplugs
- [ ] Drill and screwdriver
- [ ] Fabric
- [ ] Sewing machine, needle, thread
- [ ] Curtain rods and brackets

Patterned and pleated
An effective way to use patterned fabric on a wall: the design is a delicate one, and the fabric stops short at the dado rail. A lime green frill emphasizes the effect and picks up the green in fabric and wallpaper.

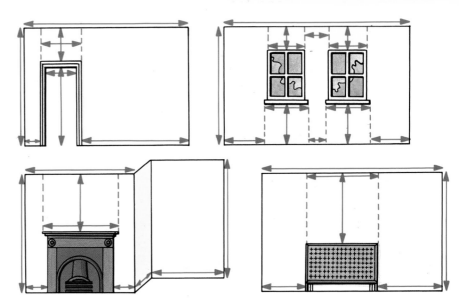

MEASURING YOUR ROOM

Before you start you need to measure up the room so that you can work out the amount of battens, the length of curtain rods and the metrage of fabric.

1 *Draw plans of the walls* ▷
Measure each wall and draw up a sketch showing all the major obstacles (windows, doors, and so on). Mark the overall measurements, with the dimensions of the obstacles. Then divide each wall into a series of rectangles, as shown by the dotted lines in the diagrams on the right.

2 *Calculate amount of battening*
If you plan to fix battens before fitting the curtain rods, measure the upper and lower edge of each rectangle to give the total length of battening required.

3 *Amount of curtain rod*
You need the same amount of curtain rod as battening. At this stage plan where the brackets are to go: position them to coincide with the corners of the rectangles. It's neater if you use the minimum number of sections of rod (see Step 1 opposite).

4 *Calculate the fabric*
For each rectangle on your plan you will need a panel of fabric 1½ times the width of the rectangle, and the same depth as the rectangle plus a total of 16cm for making up the casings.

FIXING BATTENS TO THE WALL

It is easier to fix the curtain rods accurately if you put up battens round the room first. Curtain rods have quite small screw fixings, so it is easier to screw them straight on to wood, rather than into plaster with wall plugs.

1 *Cut lengths of batten*
Consult your plan (see above) and cut lengths of batten to fit each section to be covered.

2 *Dealing with external corners* ▷
At external corners, allow for extra battening so you can extend one length to overlap the end of the adjacent length for a neat finish.

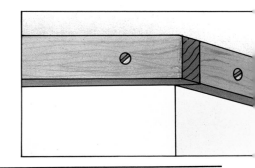

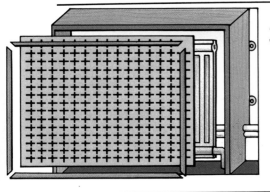

3 *Boxing in radiators* ◁
If you are going to box in your radiators you can buy custom-built covers, or build your own. Make an open box from 25×125mm planed softwood. You will need a piece for each side, scribed to fit round the skirting board at the bottom, and a piece to go across the top of the radiator. Glue and screw at the corners, strengthening the joints with angle irons

if necessary. For the front, nail fabric or decorative perforated hardboard to the outer edge of the frame, taking it down to about 10cm from floor level to allow convection currents to circulate. Glue and nail beading round the edge of the fabric or hardboard for a neat finish. Fix mirror plates to the back edges of the side panels of the box (two on each side) and screw the whole structure firmly to the wall.

4 *Organizing the electrics* ▷
Since the fabric is to be held on battens, it will stand a couple of centimetres away from the wall. The effect will be much neater if you arrange for an electrician to come and reposition the switches so they are raised from the wall. It is also advisable to move them slightly, if necessary, so that they are right at the edge of the wall – light switches up against the architrave, and sockets butting up to the skirting board. At the same time, ask the electrician to fit battens all round the sockets.

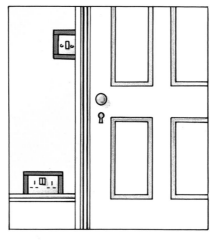

5 *Arranging pictures*
Because the fabric stands away from the wall you'll need to put up battens if you want to hang pictures. This means that the fabric is not distorted when the pictures are hung. If there are just a couple of large pictures to hang, small blocks of wood will be sufficient. If you have sets or groups of pictures to hang, long strips of batten will give you a bit of flexibility when you come to hang them.

6 Prepare the battens ◁
Fit the battens along the upper and lower edges of each area to be covered. They should be as close to the top or bottom of the rectangle as possible. Drill a series of holes, every 50cm or so down the length of the batten. Avoid fitting screws within 3cm of each end, to ensure plenty of room for fixing the rods in the corners of the rectangles.

7 Fit the battens
Hold the batten in place, mark the positions of the holes on the walls, then use a masonry bit to drill holes in the wall at each point. Fit a wallplug into each hole. Start a screw in each of the end holes in the batten, then screw them into the plugged holes. Add the intervening screws.

FIXING FABRIC WITH RODS
When fixing fabric to curtain rods there is a fair amount of straightforward sewing to be done.

1 Fix the rods in position ▷
You will need to fix curtain rods to hold the fabric at the top and bottom of each section of wall to be covered. Where there are more than two lengths of curtain rod, fit brackets back to back so that they are as nearly as possible continuous. Fit the brackets so that the middle of the bracket is about 3cm from the upper and lower edges of the wall.

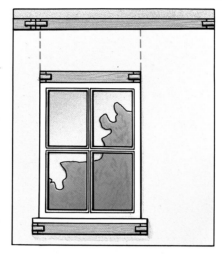

2 Make up panels with casings ▷
Cut sufficient lengths of fabric to make up the width you need. Join widths of fabric where necessary with a flat seam, pressed open. Turn under a 1cm double hem down each long edge. For the casings, turn under 3cm, then a further 5cm, and press. Make two lines of straight machine stitching, one 2cm from hem line, another 2.5cm inside that. At this stage, cut and finish the fabric without any allowance for small irregularities such as light switches.

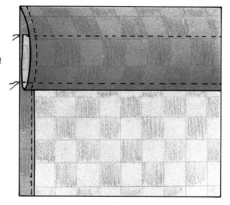

3 Fit the fabric
Thread the panels on to the curtain rods along the top of each section. Fit the rods so that the fabric panels hang down. Where there are no obstructions (such as light switches) slip the lower rods into the casings and fit the lower rods into their brackets. Distribute the fullness of the fabric evenly and bunch it up slightly at the sides so that the brackets are covered, arranging the fabric so that you don't get any unsightly gaps.

4 Small irregularities ▷
In order to make the fabric fit neatly round obstructions such as light switches, electric sockets, fireplace corners and so on, you may have to improvise slightly. Where electric sockets are close to the skirting board, fit a short length of curtain rod. Cut a piece out of the fabric where it hangs over the socket leaving 8cm allowance to make a casing. Clip into the fabric so that you can turn up a casing as before. Bind the raw edges of the fabric or turn in narrowly to neaten. At light switches, you can either cut into the fabric and staple it to battens round the switch or add short pieces of curtain rod and make casings above and below the switch.
When you have dealt satisfactorily with all the irregularities, finish fitting the fabric round the bottom of the room.

BRIGHT IDEA

WARM IT UP
For extra warmth you can insulate behind the fabric. This can be done with sheets of polystyrene, or with polyester wadding.
If you are using polystyrene, there's a choice between rolls, which are fairly thin, and stuck up like wallpaper (indeed, they are intended for hanging beneath wallpaper) or thicker sheets, which are available in 1220×2440mm panels. Make sure that the panels are no thicker than the battens. Fix the panels to the wall with one of the special adhesives made for fixing polystyrene.
If you use polyester wadding (available in 80cm widths from dressmaking departments) choose the heaviest weight and simply staple it straight to the wall so that the whole area inside the battens is completely covered.

BRIGHT IDEA

WIRED IN

For greater economy use expanding curtain wires instead of rods. Do not make the rectangles spanned by each wire too wide or there is a danger of the wires sagging in the centre. Make the casing channel slightly narrower than for curtain rods (position the rows of stitching 2cm and 3cm from the hemline). Fit screw eyes to the battens and, where panels meet, fit two screw hooks to each eye, so that you can pull the fabric panels as close together as possible.

Make sure you have the curtain wires as tightly stretched as possible, to avoid sagging.

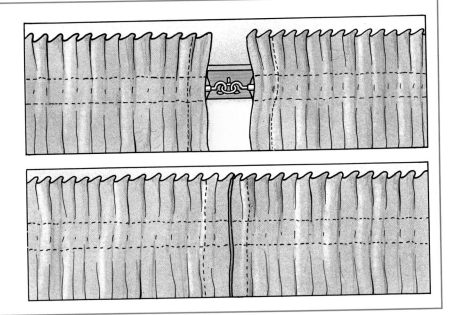

◁ **Plain and pleated**
Soft peach-coloured fabric, finely gathered, makes the perfect wallcovering for a classically elegant room. Again, the fabric ends at the dado rail. The striped paper below the rail picks up the peach tones of the fabric and echoes the vertical pleat lines above.

BASIC TILING

If you've never tried fixing ceramic tiles you'll find it's straightforward and very rewarding.

Tiles can be used in a variety of situations around the house to provide a surface that is immensely hardwearing, immune to moisture, household stains and all but the most determined physical assault. So, if you are about to have your first go at putting up tiles, here's everything you need to know about straightforward tiling.

A simple start Don't be over-ambitious. For your first project, it is wise to take on a small rectangular area of tiling supported on a level surface – for example, the splashback behind a washbasin or along the end side of a bath, or the strip of wall between a kitchen worktop and wall cupboards. You will then be able to get the feel of the technique without worrying about wasting a lot of tiles or having to master the intricacies of cutting out difficult shapes.

What kind of surface? A sound, painted surface can be left, but wallpaper or lining paper – even if it is painted – must be removed. You can tile on new plaster or plasterboard but the surface should be primed with emulsion. Don't attempt to tile on hardboard – rigid ceramic tiles may crack if applied to a flexible surface; instead, remove it and replace with chipboard or plywood. If the surface is already firmly tiled, you can stick new tiles on top.

Choosing the right size tile Tiles come in different sizes; the standard sizes are 10cm/4in and 15cm/6in square.

If you plan to tile between fixed boundaries such as worktops and wall units, choose a size that will avoid a lot of awkward cutting to size. Most suppliers will sell you a single tile that you can take home and use to check measurements and colour matching. Take accurate measurements of the area you want to tile. Then, once you know the tile size, you can work out exactly how many tiles will cover it. Count cut tiles as whole ones and buy an extra 10% to allow for breakages.

TILING EQUIPMENT

You'll need a few simple tools and pieces of equipment before you start.

Tile adhesive comes ready-mixed and the tub usually includes a notched adhesive spreader; check before you leave the store. Allow 1 litre/1lb per 1 sq m/11sq ft.

Tile grout is ready-mixed and often includes a flexible spreader. 1kg/2¼lb will grout about 6sq m/7sq yd. For a very small area you can save money by buying a combined adhesive/grout mix.

Tile cutters range from a simple carbide-tipped scoring tool to proprietary tile-cutting kits.

Pincers are used to nibble away strips of tile less than an inch wide.

A tile sander is used to smooth rough edges left by pincers.

Tile spacers – little plastic crosses you set into the adhesive bed at the corner of each tile – are optional. Whether you need them depends on the type of tile. Many tiles nowadays have slightly bevelled edges which create a uniform gap between the tiles; others have small lugs on the edges to give the same effect. Only square-edged tiles without lugs need spacers.

A spirit level is essential to check that the tiles are even.

Plain and fancy
Decorative border tiles teamed with cheaper, matching ones look very effective.

1 *Positioning a panel of tiles* ▽
With a whole panel of tiles, such as a basin splashback (below), find and pencil in the centre of the basin on the wall. Then check where the edges of the tiles will fall either by butting up the edge of the tile to the centre line (left) or by marking the centre of a tile and positioning it to match the centre of the basin (right).

CHECK YOUR NEEDS
☐ Tiles
☐ Adhesive
☐ Notched adhesive spreader
☐ Tile cutter
☐ Pincers (optional)
☐ Tile sander (optional)
☐ Tile spacers (optional)
☐ Metal rule or try-square
☐ Spirit level

☐ Grout
☐ Flexible spreader for grout
☐ Dowelling (or unsharpened end of round pencil)
☐ Silicone sealant
☐ Pencil, felt pen
☐ Sponge and dry cloths

Tiling wall to wall ▷
To tile an area wall-to-wall (top right), first lay a row of tiles loose on the surface in front of the area to be tiled and, working from the centre as for the basin splashback, position them so you have at least a third of a tile at either end. It is better to cut two tiles at each end than land up with a sliver at one end.

Tiling round a bath ▷
To tile along the end and side of a bath (right), aim to have whole tiles at either end of the run, and any cut tiles in the corner. If necessary, let the end tiles project beyond the bath rather than have a sliver to cut at the corner.

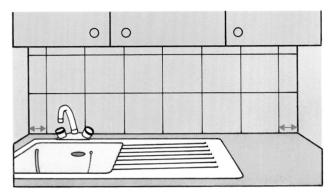

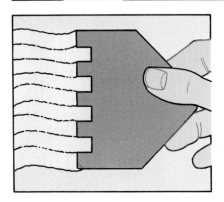

2 *Prepare the wall*
Wash down existing tiles or painted surfaces, scraping off any areas of flaking paint. Strip wallcoverings; if you are tiling only part of a papered wall, mark out and strip an area of paper 25mm/1in smaller in each direction than the tiling will occupy. Paint any bare plaster or plasterboard with emulsion.

3 *Begin with a level surface*
Use the straight edge of a basin, bath or worktop as a guideline for positioning the tiles horizontally and rest the tiles directly on the surface.

4 *Mark the start* ◁
Use the spirit level to draw a true vertical line at the point where tiling is going to start.

5 *Apply the adhesive* ◁
Scoop some tile adhesive out of the tub with the notched spreader and press it on to the wall. Draw the spreader firmly across the wall so the teeth ridge the adhesive to a standard thickness. Apply enough adhesive to allow you to position up to six tiles in the first row. Make sure you can see the vertical start line – scrape away a little adhesive if necessary.

6 *Position the first tile*
Rest the bottom edge of the tile on the worktop/basin, holding the tile at an angle of 45° to the wall (see diagram 7). Align with the vertical starting line and press the tile firmly into the adhesive. Check that it is level using the spirit level; if it isn't, twist it slightly until it is, making sure it is still aligned.

7 Adding further tiles ▷
Complete the first row in the same way, butting the tile edges closely together or fitting spacers if using square-edged tiles without lugs. If the tiling runs right up to a corner, leave any cut piece until later (but scrape off the adhesive where they will go so it doesn't set).

Check that all the tiles are sitting flush with one another; press in any that are sticking out, prise out any that have sunk too deep into the adhesive and put some more adhesive on the wall before re-bedding them.

Add further rows of whole tiles, checking that the vertical rows are correctly aligned. After placing the final row, clean off any excess adhesive.

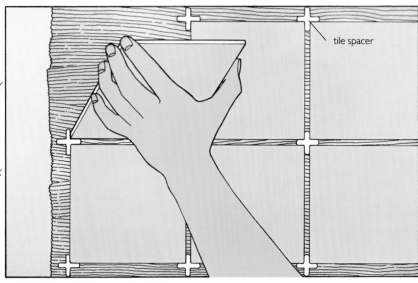

tile spacer

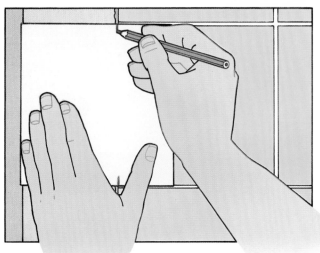

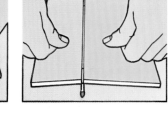

8 Fitting tiles into a corner △
To fit tiles accurately, turn the tile so that the glazed side faces the wall. Position the tile in the corner, overlapping the adjacent fixed tile; check it is straight. Mark the cutting line at top and bottom edges with a pencil, then turn the tile over and draw the line on the glazed side with a felt-tipped pen.

9 Cutting the tiles △
Cut the tile by scoring along the line on the glazed side with a tile cutter and metal rule. Place a matchstick under the tile at each end of the scored line and press firmly downwards on each half of the tile. It will snap cleanly so long as you've scored the glaze thoroughly with your tile cutter.

Test the fit of each cut tile in its gap and then spread adhesive on the back and press it into place. As a general rule, match the uncut edge of a cut tile to the edge of a whole tile. (If you plan to turn the corner and continue tiling you may be able to use the offcut along the new wall so don't throw it away.)

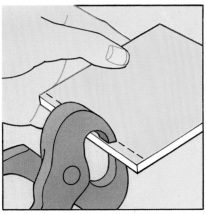

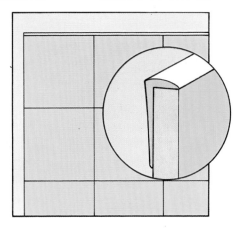

USING A CUTTER KIT
These usually consist of a tile cutter, a try-square which is used to guide the cutter, and a tool which grips the scored tile in angled jaws and snaps it along the cutting line.

CUTTING A NARROW STRIP
If you have to cut a strip of tile less than an inch wide, score it in the usual way and then use a pair of pincers to nibble off the excess tile. Use a tile sander to smooth out any unevenness on the cut edge that may result.

EDGE TRIM
You can finish off top and side edges with a tile trim. Bed the lengths of trim into the adhesive before you fix the last row of tiles and adjust the trim once they have been positioned so it fits snugly over the tile edges.

10 **Remove the spacers**
If you used tile spacers, leave the adhesive to set for at least two hours before prising them out carefully using a small screwdriver. Take care not to disturb the tiles. Scrape off any adhesive on the surface of the tiles at this stage.

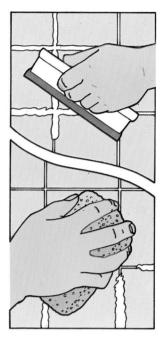

11 **Apply the grout** ▷
Leave the tile adhesive to set overnight. Then load a small amount of grout on to the flexible spreader (above) and draw it across the gaps between tiles, forcing it well in. Use a damp sponge (below) to wipe off any surplus as you complete an area of six tiles.

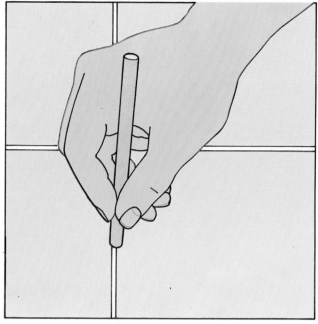

12 **Finishing off** △
Draw the end of a length of slim dowelling along each grout line to leave the surface slightly concave. Leave the grout to dry for as long as the manufacturer recommends, then polish the tile surface clean and bright with a dry cloth.

13 **Seal a splashback** ◁
Avoid leaking joints by using a flexible silicone sealant to fill narrow gaps (up to 6mm/¼in) between tiles and tops of baths of sinks. Do not use grouting as it has no elasticity and may crack with movement. First make sure the surfaces are clean and dry. Most sealants are squeezed directly from a tube. Use an even pressure and always push the tube away from you along the joint. Trim off excess sealant with a razor blade, smooth by lightly pulling a moist finger along the joint, and leave to set.

BRIGHT IDEA

COLOURED GROUTING
Most tile grout is white. If you want to add an extra touch of colour, however, you can either use coloured grout or brush on special grout paint as soon as the original white grout has dried. Matching the colour of the tiles will give a uniform look to the tiled area; a contrast colour will emphasize the tiling.

Grout paint can also be used to brighten up old grout which is beginning to look shabby.

Colours you should be able to find include red, green, pink and blue, as well as a range of neutral colours such as grey, ivory and beige.

TILING A WORK SURFACE

Finishing a worktop or vanity unit with tiles can give a completely new look to your kitchen or bathroom.

Ceramic tiles make an attractive and practical work surface for a kitchen or bathroom. They're solid, easy to clean and they should last indefinitely. The edge of the work surface can be finished with a smart matching tile trim, or with a simple timber edging.

In some ways, tiling a work surface is easier than tiling a wall: the area is relatively small, and the surface is horizontal rather than vertical. However, as tiles need to be of the thicker variety and some cutting is almost inevitable, it's advisable to have done a simple wall tiling project before, such as a washbasin splashback.

Types of surface An existing tiled or plastic laminate surface can be tiled over as long as it's clean, reasonably smooth and firmly fixed. If you're not satisfied with the surface, replace it with a piece of chipboard.

Remove a plastic or metal edging strip: a timber edging is best left in place and tiled over.

Choosing the tiles Kitchen worktops need tiles that are strong enough to withstand hard knocks and hot pans –

anything over 5mm thick is suitable, but bear in mind that the thicker the tiles, the more difficult they are to cut. You can use lighter, thinner tiles on bathroom surfaces. In general, a matt finish is better than a highly glazed one.

Wall tiles offer the greatest choice of design and colour. Purpose-made worktop tiles offer a more limited choice, but come with matching trim tiles for finishing the front edge: there are straight lengths, pairs of mitred tiles for internal corners, and special external corner pieces.

Mosaic tiles are another option: because they are small, they are easy to fit into a given area although for the same reason they're generally more fiddly to cut. It is possible to use ceramic floor tiles but they're thick and very hard to cut; quarry tiles are even thicker and, if unglazed, they must be sealed after laying.

How many tiles? Ceramic tiles are usually 10cm and 15cm square. To make sure you buy the size of tile that will fit without too much awkward cutting, it's worth buying a few to

experiment with – most suppliers will sell you single tiles. Alternatively, use cardboard cutouts and add 1mm all round to allow for the joints.

Measure the width and length of the area you want to tile. Then, once you know the size of tile you're going to use, you can calculate how many you will need. Buy enough tiles to cover the area with whole tiles, plus a few extra to allow for mistakes.

TOOLS AND EQUIPMENT

Adhesive must be waterproof. If the work surface is uneven – old tiles, for example – use a thick-bed adhesive to cover any irregularities.

Grout must be waterproof. On tiled kitchen work surfaces, where food is prepared, use an epoxy grout that is non-toxic and resists staining.

A tile cutter, with a wheel to score a cutting line and strong angled jaws to snap the tile, is the best tool for cutting thicker tiles and narrow pieces of tile.

A simple carbide-tipped scoring tool is cheaper and will do the job as long as the tiles are not too thick, and not much cutting is involved.

Tile nibblers, with tungsten-carbide jaws, are good for cutting small pieces of tile. They're easier to use on thick tiles than ordinary pincers.

A tile sander or coarse glasspaper for smoothing edges of cut tiles.

Kitchen update
Tiles look luxurious and provide a durable surface that is easy to wipe clean. Here, special postformed trim tiles are used along kitchen worktop edges for a neat, professional finish.

CHECK YOUR NEEDS

- ☐ Tiles
- ☐ Trim tiles OR
  timber edging strip plus adhesive and panel pins
- ☐ Waterproof tile adhesive
- ☐ Notched adhesive spreader
- ☐ Tile spacers (for tiles without lugs)
- ☐ Tile cutter
- ☐ Tile nibblers or pincers
- ☐ Tile sander or glasspaper
- ☐ Waterproof epoxy grout
- ☐ Flexible grout spreader or cloth
- ☐ Silicone sealant
- ☐ Wooden battens, about 25 × 50mm
- ☐ Hammer and panel pins
- ☐ Metal rule
- ☐ Pencil and felt tip pen
- ☐ Old cloths or sponge

1 *Plan the layout* ▽ ▷
Work out the best layout for tiling by loose-laying the whole surface and adjusting the tiles until they look right. If using square-edged tiles without lugs, fit tile spacers in between to allow for joints.

Keep cut tiles to the back of the worktop, and try to avoid narrow pieces of tile as they are difficult to cut.

The front edge How you finish the front edge of the work surface determines how you arrange the rest of the tiles.

If you're having a tiled edging (left), take into account the width of the trim tiles when laying out the whole tiles.

If you plan to have a timber edging (right), butt the whole tiles up to the front edge of the surface.

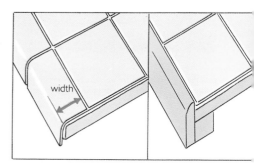
width

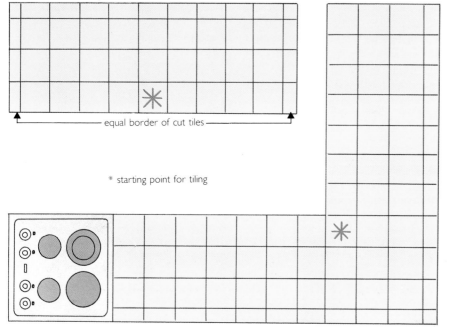
— equal border of cut tiles —

* starting point for tiling

Tiling a rectangular shape Find and mark the centre of the front edge of the work surface. Then match the centre of a tile to this mark, and lay a row of loose tiles all along the front edge. If the work surface is open at both ends, adjust the tiles so that you have an equal border of cut tiles at each end. If it is open only at one end, place full tiles here and cut tiles along the walls.

Once the layout is fixed, mark the position of the centre front row tile (*) as the starting point for tiling.

Tiling an L-shape For an L-shaped work surface, position a tile at the internal corner (*) and pencil round the edges to mark where tiling is going to start. As you cannot adjust the starting point, you may have to cut tiles to fit on exposed edges.

2 *Prepare the base*
Wash down existing laminate or tiles, and rub over with abrasive paper to give a good key for the new tile adhesive. Lift tiles that are loose or uneven and refix with new adhesive; fill any cracks and holes with all-purpose cellulose filler. Paint a new chipboard base with several coats of undercoat to seal it.

The front edge of the work surface should be the same depth as, or just less than, the depth of your chosen finish. If it's not, glue and screw a timber batten to the underside of the front edge, making sure that it doesn't obstruct any drawers or cupboard doors below.

3 *Begin with a straight edge* ▷
Use a timber batten along the front of the work surface as a guideline for positioning the first row of tiles in a straight line. Otherwise the layout is likely to end up askew.

If using a tiled edging (above right), mark a line along the front of the work surface to allow for the width of the trim tiles – these are laid last. Hold a straight piece of trim, short side vertical, against the edge of the work surface; make a series of pencil marks along the top edge of the tile and join them up with a straight line. Then loosely nail a timber batten up to the pencil line and use this as the edge for laying whole tiles.

With a timber edging (below right), tack the batten to the edge of the work surface so that it projects above the surface by the thickness of a tile.

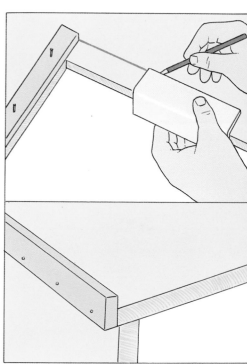

4 *Start tiling* ▷
With your starting point in mind (see Step 1), apply enough adhesive with a notched spreader to lay four or five tiles along the front edge.

Lay the key tile (*) first, butting it against the batten, and press gently but firmly into place. Add the next tile alongside – butting edges together or fitting spacers if necessary – and continue along the row until you can't fit any more whole tiles. Check all the time that tiles are accurately aligned with each other; if the layout starts going askew and is not corrected, the error will get progressively worse.

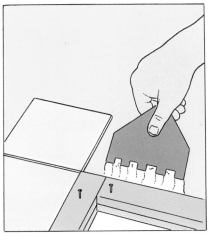

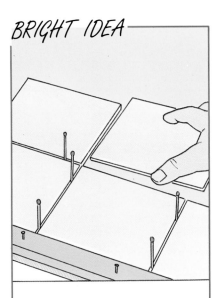

TILE SPACERS △
Substitute matchsticks for special tile spacers when laying square-edged tiles without lugs. Use two at each tile edge, and remove before grouting the joins.

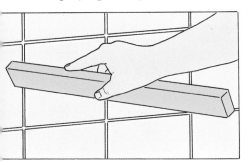

5 *Add further tiles* ◁
Spread more adhesive and continue laying rows of full tiles, working back to the wall as far as you can go. Leave cut border tiles until last, but scrape off any adhesive in the area where they are going before it dries.

From time to time, press the tiles down with a batten as shown to make sure that the surface is level.

6 *Mark border tiles*
Mark and cut border tiles individually to make sure that they fit the gaps between whole tiles and the wall, for example.

To mark a tile to fit, hold it glazed side down with one edge against the wall, and mark two points on the sides of the tile where the cutting line will be. Then turn the tile over and use a rule and felt-tip pen to draw a line on to the glazed side.

7 *Cut border tiles*
Hold a metal rule firmly against the cutting line and score along it deeply with a tile cutter.

Thick tiles, and very narrow pieces of tile, are best cut using a pair of tile snappers with angled jaws. Otherwise, put a matchstick under each end of the scored line and press firmly downwards on each side with your fingertips – if you feel resistance, score the line

deeper and try again. If border tiles are almost full-size, score a line in the usual way and nibble off the excess tile with pincers or nibblers. Smooth rough edges with a tile sander or glasspaper.

Test each tile for fit, then spread adhesive on to the work surface and press the tile into place with the cut edge to the wall. If the space is narrow, it's often easier to apply adhesive to the back of the tile instead of the surface.

8 *Fix the edging* ▽
Once the work surface has been completely tiled, remove the batten and finish the edge with special trim tiles or with a length of timber moulding.

A tiled edge Spread adhesive on to work surface and undersides of tiles, and position tiles so that joints align with those between whole tiles.

To lay the tiles, begin at an internal corner with the mitred tiles (below left). Then work out from the corner, laying the straight trim pieces (middle): if necessary, cut tiles to fit by scoring the surface deeply with a tile cutter and nibbling the waste away with pincers or tile nibblers. At external corners, fix a special corner piece (right) – it may be necessary for you to cut a small piece

off the work surface to make the tile fit as neatly as possible.

A timber edge Cut moulding to fit. Fix with woodworking adhesive and reinforce with panel pins, punching the heads in and filling recesses with wood filler. Follow Steps 9-11 overleaf, then seal wood with two or three coats of varnish or paint it to match the tiles.

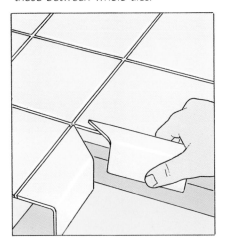

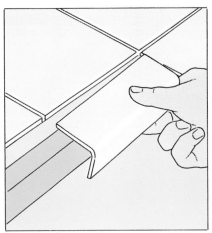

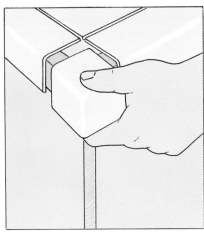

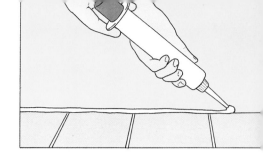

9 Remove tile spacers

If you are using tile spacers (or matchsticks), leave the adhesive for an hour or two so that it sets firm before prising them out carefully with a small screwdriver.

Rub off any adhesive on the tile surface with a damp cloth, taking care not to dislodge the tiles.

10 Apply the grout

Leave tiles for 24 hours before grouting. Using a flexible spreader or cloth, rub grout into the gaps between tiles (except where work surface tiles meet a sink or tiles on a wall).

Wipe off any splodges of grout on the tiles with a damp cloth before it dries, and run a round-ended stick along each joint to smooth the grout and leave the surface slightly concave. Leave grout to dry, then polish the tile surface with a soft dry cloth.

11 Use a sealant △

Use a flexible silicone sealant to seal the join where tiles meet with a sink or basin, and to fill the gap between work surface and wall.

CUTTING AWKWARD SHAPES

Most cut tiles will have simple straight edges, but you may have to make a few odd-shape cuts to fit tiles round external corners or round obstacles such as hobs and sinks. Don't fit tiles too tightly round a hob – allow a joint space as usual so that, as temperatures change, they can expand and contract without cracking.

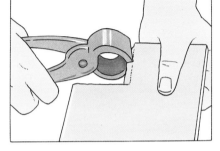

Cutting a curve ▷

Make a tile-sized template from card or paper. Hold it in place against the curved object, and make a series of cuts in the edge with scissors or a sharp knife so that it can be folded to the shape of the curve.

Then cut the curved shape out of the card, place the template on the tile and mark and score the outline. Score a grid of lines on the waste side of the line and nibble away small pieces with pincers or tile nibblers until the line is reached. If necessary, smooth the cut edge with a tile sander.

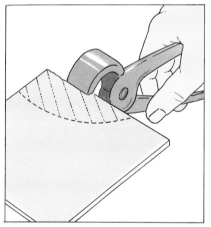

Cutting L-shaped corner tiles △

Starting on one side of the corner, put the tile to be cut on top of the last whole tile laid before the wall. Then put another tile on top, but with its edge against the wall. Draw a cutting line across the middle tile, using the top one as a profile.

Slide the tiles round the corner and repeat on the other side of the angle. Join up the marked lines to form the L-shape and score them with a tile cutter. Then score a grid of lines over the waste area and nibble this away with pincers or nibblers.

Patchwork picture ◁

An odd collection of tiles can be put together to great effect, as long as they're linked in some way – by colour, pattern or style.

Here, a beautiful collection of antique tiles in warm, tawny colours makes a vivid patchwork of different floral designs on a kitchen worktop. Look out for similar tiles on market stalls and in local junk shops.

TILING A ROOM

Tiling large areas is no more difficult
than small ones so long as
you are prepared to plan ahead
carefully before you start.

The best way to practise your tiling skills if you've never done any before is by covering just a small area such as a washbasin splashback or a worktop. See Basic Tiling and Tiling A Work Surface, pages 79-86, for the basic techniques of setting out the area and fixing, cutting and grouting tiles.

When you are tackling a larger area – a whole wall, or perhaps even a complete room – you use exactly the same techniques; the big difference is the sheer scale of the job, which makes the preliminary setting out the most important part. The problem is that unless you have absolutely plain walls, there will be a number of obstacles to tile round. You have to decide how to get the best fit round them with the inflexible tile squares, without having to cut impossibly thin slivers to fill in all the gaps.

You may also want to tile awkward shapes such as the window recesses, or things like bath surrounds. Here extra care is essential if you are to get professional-looking results.

Last, you may want to add decorative trims – wood, plastic or metal edgings, for example – to finish off your newly-tiled areas. And then there's the problem of putting back the various wall-mounted fittings which you had to take down to do the tiling in the first place.

TOOLS AND EQUIPMENT

You will need the same basic tool kit here as you did for tiling small areas – see Check Your Needs overleaf. In addition, for whole-wall tiling you will need some long straight timber battens to act as supports and guides, masonry nails plus a claw hammer to enable you to fit them temporarily to the walls, and a spirit level to ensure that the battens are fixed absolutely horizontal. You will also need a surprisingly large number of tiles for even quite a small wall. Measure up accurately, counting all part tiles as whole ones, and allowing 10% extra for breakages. Also make sure that you have enough adhesive and grout to finish the job; nothing is more annoying than running out of adhesive with just a few tiles left to fix. Always use waterproof adhesive and grout for wet areas such as kitchens and bathrooms.

Ceramic tiles have to be laid with a small gap all round to allow for expansion. Formerly this was achieved either by using tiles made with a small projection, or lug, on each side; or by inserting spacers while putting them up.

But many tiles nowadays are of the universal type, with no spacer lugs but bevelled edges which achieve the same effect. They are glazed on two adjacent edges and so can be used at exposed edges or corners when necessary. The old-fashioned special tiles with one or two rounded and glazed edges (RE and REX tiles) are now seldom found.

Some cheaper tile ranges have edges that are erratically and poorly glazed, with just a few tiles in each box having two completely glazed edges. If you need tiles with glazed edges of good quality for finishing off part-tiled walls and external corners, check this point.

If you will have to drill holes in your new tiles to replace wall fixings make sure you have sharp masonry drill bits, wall plugs and some masking tape to help you drill the holes accurately.

Strategic stripes
This well-planned tiling has striped tiles lining up with the sill line at the window and creating a skirting board effect at floor level. A timber trim in matching blue completes the picture.

PLANNING THE LAYOUT

If you're planning to tile or half-tile a complete wall or room, the most important thing to do is to plan precisely where the tiles will fall. You will need to look carefully at each wall and any features such as windows and doors to help you decide how to arrange the tiles.

A skilled tiler will use a batten marked out in tile widths to work this out, but for the beginner it's easier to use the actual tiles for a simple layout.

1 Planning a plain wall ▷
On a plain, uninterrupted wall this is quite straightforward. You start at the centre bottom of the area to be tiled and work outwards and upwards from this point.

Measure across the wall and pencil on the centre point. Centre the first tile on this mark – either prop it against the wall or lay it on the floor. Lay out more tiles in each direction until you cannot get any more in. If the gaps left at each side are very small move the centre mark to the left or right until they are at least one quarter of a tile wide. This is because narrow pieces not only look ugly but are very hard to cut. If your tiles are square-edged, insert slips of card between them to represent the joint spacings.

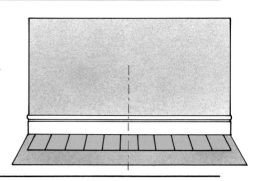

2 Planning the verticals
Once you have established how the tiles are to run horizontally, check what's going to happen vertically. Hold a tile against one of the side walls at the skirting board or floor. Pencil tile widths up to the finishing point. If this results in an awkwardly narrow piece at the ceiling or the top row of half-tiling is not where you want it to be, use a cut tile at the bottom of the wall instead of a whole one.

3 Coping with a window ▷
If there is a window, centre the tiles horizontally on it rather than the wall – some narrow pieces may be inevitable and are less conspicuous in corners. When planning the vertical layout, arrange the tiles so that complete ones coincide with the sill level, but not if this means having very narrow cut pieces at the top. Repeat process on the other walls; take care to start from the same bottom line on each one.

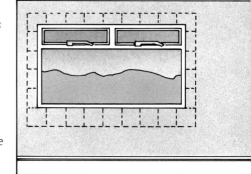

PREPARING TO TILE

With large areas of tiling three things are vital. First, the walls must be sound and flat. Second, the tile rows must be precisely horizontal. If they're not, errors will accumulate as you tile across the wall, throwing the verticals out of alignment with disastrous results. And if you're tiling right round a room, inaccurate levels will mean that your rows don't match up at the starting and finishing point. Third, the tiles need some support while the adhesive sets. Without it the whole tiled area could slump down the wall.

1 Prepare the walls
To give a sound surface to tile over, strip off any wall-covering. Then fill any cracks and depressions with a proprietary cellulose filler. Existing tiles can be tiled over provided that they are firmly stuck to the wall and the new joints come in different places.

2 Fix the battens ▷
To get the tiles horizontal, and to support them while the adhesive is drying, you have to fix a line of battens across the wall (or right round the room) just above skirting board or floor level, securing them with partly-driven masonry nails so you can remove them later. The precise level will be dictated by your plan, but will usually be between half and three-quarters of a tile width above the skirting board or floor. Don't rely on these being level; they probably won't be. Draw the level in pencil first, using your spirit level, and then nail the battens up and check the battens are level as you go.

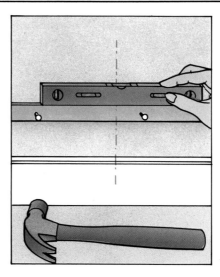

3 Tiling over tiles
If you're tiling over existing tiles you will have to drill holes through them for the masonry nails which will hold the battens in place. Drill fine pilot holes in a batten, hold it up to the wall and drill through one batten hole into the tiling. Pin this end in place, then swing the batten up, check it is horizontal with the spirit level and drill through its other end, ready for nailing.

TILING THE WALL

With all the battens in place you can start tiling.

1 Find the starting point
Refer to your pencil mark to see where your starting point is: the centre of the wall, or some other point. Transfer the mark on to the batten. You can if you wish fit a vertical guide batten at one side, but it's not strictly necessary; a true horizontal base line will ensure that your verticals are true too so long as you place the tiles carefully.

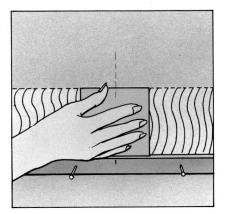

2 Apply the adhesive ◁
Apply a band of adhesive to the wall and fit the first row of whole tiles, adding tile spacers at the top corners if necessary. Then carry on up the wall, fitting whole tiles until you reach an obstacle such as a window opening. Carry on tiling up the wall at each side of it, until you reach the top of half-tiling, or the last whole row of whole tiles beneath the ceiling. Remember to leave spaces for items such as soap dishes or for a mirror (see Bright Idea overleaf).

3 Set in any trim
If you're using a plastic or metal tile trim to finish off a half-tiled area, bed its rear flange in the adhesive before fitting the top row of tiles (see overleaf). Do not fit cut tiles at the side and top edges at this stage.

4 Tile above openings ▷
Where tiles are to be fixed over a recessed window opening, you will need another support batten. Fix it to the wall over the opening with its top edge in line with the top edge of the whole tiles you placed earlier at each side of the opening. Then carry on tiling as before, placing whole tiles up to ceiling level. Leave all the battens in place for at least 24 hours to allow the adhesive to set hard.

5 Fit the cut tiles ◁
Next day carefully prise out the masonry nails holding the battens in place, using a claw hammer, and remove the battens. Prise out any tile spacers at this stage too. Mark and cut tiles to fit the space between the skirting board or floor and fix them in position. It's easier to spread adhesive on the back of each cut piece with the notched spreader than to try to apply it to the narrow section of exposed wall.

Then fit cut tiles at each side of the wall, and between the last row of whole tiles and the ceiling if the tiling is full height positioning the cut edge of each tile against the ceiling.

If you have tiled more than one wall, fill in the cut pieces on each wall. Make sure that there is a slight gap between adjacent cut corner pieces to allow for any slight movement in the house structure. If the pieces are a tight fit this could crack them.

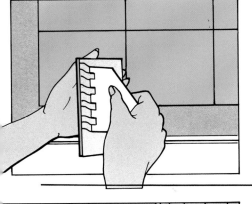

6 Tile window recesses ◁
The next step is to tile any window recesses, shelves or boxes concealing pipework. Start by cutting tiles to fit the gap left on the face of the wall between the last row of whole tiles and the edges of the recess. Then fix whole tiles to the sill, sides and head of the opening so their glazed edges neatly overlap the cut edges of the tiles you just placed. If the recess is shallow, cut them down at the

back edges to fit. If you are tiling the 'ceiling' or head of the window recess, you may need to rig up a temporary support – a batten and props wedged between head and sill – to support the tiles. Finally, on a deep recess, fit cut pieces between the whole tiles and the window frame to complete the recess.

7 Tiling external corners ◁
A similar overlap to the one round a window recess is formed at external corners. The rule here is to have the tile with the exposed, glazed edge on the more prominent wall.

If you are tiling three adjacent surfaces – on a fully tiled, boxed-in bath surround, for example – the overlap at the external corner cannot be accommodated without a gap equal to the thickness of a tile being left on the

top. This will not be noticeable when filled with grout. Position the tiles as shown in the diagram, so that the horizontal corner tile covers the edges of the top two vertical tiles laid below it.

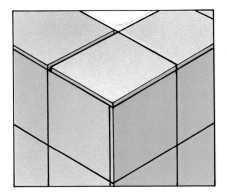

FINISHING THE JOB

After all the tiling has been completed, the trims, grouting and accessories have to be added to give the finishing touches to the job.

1 Add the trim

As mentioned earlier, you can finish off tiled areas and external corners neatly with special plastic or metal tile trims which give a neat, rounded edge. Cut them to length with a fine-toothed hacksaw, mitring the corners in a mitre box if framing a window reveal or similar opening. Bed the trim in the tile adhesive before placing the final row of tiles over the trim's back flange and carefully tap the trim in place so it sits flush with the tile edges.

2 Add accessories ▷

If you are adding matching ceramic accessories such as soap dishes and toilet roll holders, leave spaces in the ordinary tiling and wipe away the adhesive. Next day, when fitting the cut tiles, butter some adhesive on to the back of the accessory and set it in place. Use masking tape to support it while the adhesive 'grabs'.

3 Grout the tiles

Leave the tiling overnight for the adhesive to set. Then grout all the gaps using a flexible plastic spreader. Wipe off excess grout with a damp cloth as you work, and round off the grout lines with a piece of slim dowelling. When the grout is dry, polish the tile surfaces

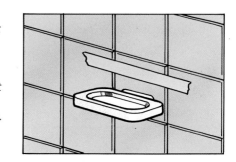

with a clean dry cloth to remove smears.

It's best not to grout internal angles since movement in the house structure could cause cracking. Use silicone sealant instead, which remains flexible.

4 Replace fittings

If you have screw-mounted wall fittings such as mirrors and shelves to replace once tiling is complete, stick masking tape to the tile surface and mark the fixing positions on it. The tape prevents the drill bit from skating away from the mark. Use a sharp masonry drill bit and a slow speed setting on the drill, pressing lightly until the bit bites through the tile glaze. Then drill the hole to the required depth. Remove the tape, insert the wall plug and make the fixing. In a really wet area such as a shower cubicle put a bead of silicone sealant round the screw shank as you drive it in to stop water seeping behind the tiles.

BRIGHT IDEA

Fitting a mirror If you want to have mirrors in the bathroom you can simply screw them to the tiled wall with mirror screws. The only drawback is that steam can affect the silvering if it reaches the back of the mirror. To get round this, fit the mirror flush with the tiles. To make sure of a perfect fit (and save on tiles) leave a space for it when hanging the tiles, then measure the area and order a mirror of that size from a glass merchant. Stick it to the wall with adhesive pads or blobs of epoxy resin adhesive. Seal the join between mirror and tiles with silicone sealant. Stick masking tape to the edge of the mirror while applying the sealant to it so that you don't smear the surface.

◁ **Carefully colourful**
Multi-coloured tiles used here emphasize the importance of laying them in the correct way round a recessed window. The alternating pink, grey and green tiles are not only centred on the window but the dominant pink colour appears in the centre and at all four corners.

INDEX

A

Acrylic colours
  for murals, 58
  for stencilling, 49
Air bubbles in wallpaper,
  treatment of, 67
Anaglypta, 69, 72, 73

B

Bathrooms, tiling, 84-6, 91
Battens
  used in fabric lining, 80, 81
  used in tiling, 92
Borders
  anaglypta, 72
  stencilled, 51-2
  wallpaper, 64
Brushes see Paintbrushes

C

Ceiling roses, 68
Ceilings
  decorating, 65-8
  painting, 13-16
  stencilled borders, 52
Ceramic tiles see Tiling
China, spattering, 30
China paint 29-30
Cissing, 29-32, 38
Colour combination, using
  spattering, 29
Colour shading, 25-8
Colour washing, 25-7
  base for murals, 58
Combing, 41, 44
Cork wallcoverings, 74
Corners
  fixing cornices and coving round, 77
  papering round, 64
  tiling round, 84-5, 90
Cornices, 75-8
  painting, 78
  repairing and restoring, 78
  stripping, 78
Coving, 75-8
Cracks see Filler
Curtain rods, used with fabric, 79-82
Curtain wires, used with fabric, 82
Cutting in, 19

D

Dado rail, 72, 82
Designs for stencils, 53-6
Distemper, recreating effect of, 25
  removal, 7, 8, 26
Doors
  painting, 20, 47
  papering round, 64
  special effects, 43
Dragging, 41-3

E

Edges, protection whilst painting, 19

Eggshell paints, 11-12
  for cissing, 31
  for colour shading, 25-7
  for dragging or combing, 42
  for marbling, 34
  for murals, 58
  for ragging and rag-rolling, 21-4
  for spattering, 30
  for stencilling, 49
  for stippling, 21-4
  for tortoiseshelling, 38
  on wallcoverings, 69, 71
Emulsion paints, 11-12
  for colour washing, 25-8
  for murals, 58
  for spattering, 30
  sponging, 16
  for stencilling, 49
  on wallcoverings, 69
Enamel, spattering, 30
Equipment, for painting
  see Tools and equipment
    for painting

F

Fabric, spattering, 32
Fabric wallcoverings, 74, 79-82
Filler
  for cracks and holes, 8, 10, 18
Fittings and accessories
  for tiled walls, 94
Flicking, 32
Flock wallcoverings, 74
Foam polyethylene wallcoverings, 74
Foil wallcoverings, 74
Fossilizing see Cissing
Frames, tortoiseshell
  for pictures and mirrrors, 37, 40
Frieze, ceiling, 51-2
Furnishings, protection during
  decoration, 7, 8, 9, 13

G

Glass
  paint smudges
    prevention, 45-6
    removal, 20
  spattering, 30
Glaze
  for cissing, 30-1
  for combing, 44
  for dragging, 42-3
  for marbling, 34-5
  for murals, 58
  for ragging, rag-rolling, 21-2, 24
  for scumbling, 71-2
  for spattering, 30-1
  for stippling, 21-3
Gloss paints, 11-12, 17-19
  for murals, 58
  for spattering, 30
  on wallcoverings, 69, 71
Grout paint, 86
Grouting, 86, 90, 94

H

Hessian wallcoverings, 74
Highlights on walls, 28

I

Insulation, behind fabric, 81

K

Kitchen, tiling, 84-6
Knots, treatment of, 18, 30

L

Light fittings
  concealed in cornice, 78
  fixing, 68
  papering round, 67
Lincrusta, 69, 70-1, 73
Lining paper, 13, 61, 70, 73
  base for murals, 58
  cross-lining, 64

M

Marbling, 33-6
Masking tape, 46-8
Metal, preparation for painting, 11-12
Mirrors and tiled surface, 94
Mitre box, 76
Mosaic tiles, 87
Moulding, 75-8
Mould treatment, 7, 8, 10
Murals, 57-60

O

Oil-based paints, 11-12, 13, 15
  see also Eggshell paints, Gloss paints

P

Paintbrushes, 14, 15
  see also Tools and equipment
    for painting
  care of, 18
  cutting-in, 19, 45
  for dragging, 41
  for murals, 58
  for stencilling, 49, 51
  for stippling, 21, 23, 27
Painting
  edges, 45
  spray gun, 48
  walls, surface preparation, 7, 8
  wood, 45-7
Paint pad, 14, 15, 45-6
Paint roller, 14
Paints and primers, choosing for
  interior use, 11-12
    see also Eggshell, Emulsion, Gloss,
      Oil-based paints
  amount required, 13, 18
  textured, removal, 8
Paint tins, management, 19
Papering see Wallpapering
Pasting see Wallpapering
Patterns, painted, 48
Pictures, hanging
  on fabric-lined wall, 80
Pipework, concealing with cornice, 75
Plaster, cornices, 75
Plasterboard, coving, 75
Plaster surface
  new, preparation, 7, 70
  repair of, 10
Plastic foam, expanded, coving, 75

Polyester wadding,
    for wall insulation, 81
Polystyrene
    coving, 75
    for wall insulation, 81
Preparation of decorating surfaces, 7-10
Primers, 11-12, 19, 23, 30

Q

Quarry tiles, 87

R

Radiators
    boxing in, 80
    management, for fabric lining, 80-1
    papering round, 64
Rag-rolling, 21-4
Ragging, 21-4
    marbling, 34-6
Relief wallcoverings, 69-72, 73
Rot, in wood, 17

S

Safety, electrical, 8
Scotia moulding, 75
Scumble glaze see Glaze
Sealant
    for baths and sinks, 86, 90
    for internal angles, 94
Sizing, 8, 61, 65
Skirting boards, painting, 47
Sockets
    management, for fabric lining, 80-1
    papering round, 64
Solvents and thinners, 12
Spacers, for tiling, 86, 89-90
Spattering, 29-32
Sponging, 16
    base for murals, 58
Spray painting, 48
Stainers, 22
Starting-points
    painting walls and ceilings, 15
    painting woodwork, 17, 20
    papering, 62, 66
    ragging, 24

stippling, 23
tiling, 84, 88, 92-3
Stencilling, 49-56
Stencils,
    DIY, 53-6
    used for murals, 60
Stippling, 21-3, 27-8
    base for murals, 58
Stripper, steam
    see Wallpapering, stripping
Stripping, cornices, 78
Superdurable (Superglypta), 69, 73
Switches
    management, for fabric lining, 80-1
    papering round, 64

T

Textured paint, 12
Thinners and solvents, 12
Tiles, drilling holes, 94
Tiling
    rooms, 91-4
    walls, 83-6
    work surfaces, 87-90
Tinting, with stainers, 22
Tools and equipment
    for cissing, 30
    for colour washing and shading, 26
    for fabric lining, 79
    for fixing cornices and coving, 76
    for making stencils, 53
    for painting, 8, 14, 45-6
    for papering, 61, 65
    for spattering, 30
    for tiling, 83, 87, 91
Tortoiseshelling, 37-40
Trims,
    to edge tiled surfaces, 88-9, 93, 94
Trompe l'oeil effects, 57

U

Undercoat, 11-12

V

Varnishing
    after dragging or combing, 42-4

after marbling, 34-6
after spattering, 30
after stencilling, 49
in tortoiseshelling, 38-9
Veins
    in marbling, 34-6
    in spattering, 31
Vinyl silk emulsion, 22
Vinyl wallcoverings, 69, 74

W

Wallcoverings, 73-4
    fabric, 74, 79-82
    printed or PVC coated, 73
    quantity needed, 62, 66
    relief, 69-72
    woodchip, 73
Wallpapering, 61-72, 73-4
    stripping, 7-10
    surface preparation, 7, 9
Walls
    see Wallcoverings, Wallpapering
    childproof, 71
    painting, 13-16
        special effects, 21-30
            see also names of specific effects
    surface preparation, 7-10, 11-12
    tiling, 83-4, 91-2
Water-based paint, 11-12
    see also Emulsion paint
Window frames
    painting, 20, 45-6
    papering round, 64
    tiling round, 92, 93
Wiring, concealing with cornice, 75, 78
Wood
    cornices, 75
    preparation for painting, 11-12, 18
Woodchip paper, 73
Woodwork, painting
    special effects, 30, 33, 41-4, 58
    surface preparation, 17-19, 30
Work surfaces, tiling, 83-6
Worktop tiles, 83-6

PHOTOGRAPHIC CREDITS
Front cover Camargue, 1 Stencil-itis, 2-3 Dulux, 4-5 Steve Tanner/Eaglemoss, 6 Dulux, 7 Dulux, 13 Dulux, 16 PWA International, 17 Dulux, 21 & 23 Dorma, 23(main picture) Chris Stephens/Eaglemoss, 24(inset) Crown Paints, 24(main picture) Chris Stephens/Eaglemoss, 25 EWA/A von Einsiedel, 28 Shona Wood/Eaglemoss, 29 La Maison de Marie Claire/Eriaud/Comte, 32 Simon Butcher/Eaglemoss, 33 EWA/Tom Leighton, 36 Dulux, 37 Freda Parker/Eaglemoss, 40 Simon Butcher/Eaglemoss, 41 Dulux, 42 Mr Tomkinson, 45 Dulux, 48 Crown Paints, 49 Stencil Ease at Carolyn Warrender, 51 EWA/Spike Powell, 53 Crown Paints, 56 Cover Plus from Woolworths, 57 EWA/Michael Dunne, 60 Jean-Paul Bonhommet, 61 PWA International, 66 EWA/Michael Dunne, 68 Aristocast, 69 Crown Paints, 72 Crown Paints, 75 Dulux, 78 PWA International, 79 Textra, 82 Textra, 83 Sara Taylor/Eaglemoss, 86 Winchmore Ltd, 87 Cristal Tiles, 90 EWA/Jerry Tubby, 91 Cristal Tiles, 94 Elizabeth Ann Kitchens